Rebounding From Childbirth

Rebounding From Childbirth

Toward Emotional Recovery

Lynn Madsen

Bergin & Garvey
Westport, Connecticut • London

Library of Congress Cataloging-in-Publication Data

Madsen, Lynn.
    Rebounding from childbirth: Toward emotional recovery / Lynn Madsen.
        p.   cm.
    Includes bibliographical references and index.
    ISBN 0–89789–348–4 (alk. paper : pb)
    1. Postpartum depression. 2. Grief therapy. 3. Labor
(Obstetrics)—Complications—Psychological aspects. 4. Childbirth—
Psychological aspects. 5. Self-help techniques. I. Title.
RG852.M335 1994
618.7′6—dc20   93–40162

British Library Cataloguing in Publication Data is available.

Library of Congress Catalog Card Number: 93–40162
ISBN: 0–89789–348–4

First published in 1994

Bergin & Garvey, 88 Post Road West, Westport, CT 06881
An imprint of Greenwood Publishing Group, Inc.

Printed in the United States of America

The paper used in this book complies with the
Permanent Paper Standard issued by the National
Information Standards Organization (Z39.48–1984).

10 9 8 7 6 5 4 3 2 1

Copyright Acknowledgment

The author and publisher gratefully acknowledge permission to use excerpts from American Psychiatric Association: *Diagnostic and Statistical Manual of Mental Disorders, Third
Edition, Revised*, Washington, DC, American Psychiatric Association, 1987.

To Katie Louise

CONTENTS

ACKNOWLEDGMENTS

This book would not have been born without my faithful writing group. Thank you Bea Pieper who encouraged me to sign the contract and write it at all. Thank you Roseann Giguere who cleared the manuscript of dangling participles and dubbed me the original "woman who, dangling from the ceiling, saw a spider." Thank you Bea Liu who gave me expert literary feedback, and wisdom about babies, recalling her own childbirth experiences from her eighty-six year old vantage. And thank you Barb Schubring, copy editor extraordinaire and mentor of computer desktop publishing.

Thank you friends who read and gave feedback on early drafts of the manuscript: Lynn Collins, Nancyanna Dill, Allison Ek, Chris Freedman, Dr. Susan Green, Sally Kirwin, and Deb Roberts. Thank you to all the women who have shared their birth stories, who have provided comfort, inspiration, and encouragement.

Thank you and blessings to my family—Michael, Evan, Kyle, and just-born Katherine, who are my wellspring of love and the best reasons for this book.

INTRODUCTION

I write with two voices; I have a Ph.D. in psychology, and work with women and couples who have experienced traumatic births or unexpected birth outcomes, processing the upheavals of every possible emotion. I am also a mother, who has birthed babies in two very, very different ways. The first birth was cesarean because of a prolapsed cord; the second was a successful hospital VBAC (vaginal birth after cesarean) with no episiotomy, no drugs, and a nine and a half pound baby pushed down the pike.

Both voices give perspective to this book. As a mother, I searched bookshelves for this book. That is why it was written; I needed to read it. The book was originally written entirely as a memoir. I tried to keep my personal story and journey separate from my professional life. But the publisher asked me to blend the two, and eventually I sat down at the computer with all aspects of myself present.

Second, as a professional psychotherapist, through my own experience of a traumatic birth, I developed keen awareness of when a birth event needed attention, both with individuals and between couples. Eventually, I began to see clients specifically for this issue, receiving referrals from clients' friends, clinics, birth educators, and special-interest groups that help people deal with grief, trauma, and loss.

Through these words, I want to help any other woman heal from her birth experience. If she does, then I have done my job. I hope you as a reader can hear both voices: the professional therapist, and the mother who has found her way through the healing journey and continues to do so.

Each woman is an expert about herself; each mother is an expert about birth. What a woman may discover from this book is that although someone with more education, in particular, medical training, might have her best interests in mind, she herself still must be the judge of how she wants to be treated. Many medical experts tell us what they think we need, and we do not question their advice. Then we doubt our own sanity and abilities after some procedure is done. Each woman needs to decide for herself what her birth means to her, how she needs to heal, and how she will integrate her birth experience into the rest of her life.

The book can be read in various ways. It can be read cover to cover, or skipped through to read personal accounts or sections on a specific topic. By using the "work on your own" sections at the end of each chapter, a woman can gather her own evidence and choose appropriate tools for her particular path of healing.

Parts of my own story are woven into the book, for I know my own story best and can relate it most clearly. I have also included four other women's stories. Some women may not have access to hearing others' birth stories; listening and telling is a vital part of healing. While writing this book, with each conversation about it, I was given examples a friend, colleague, hairdresser, or client wanted to have included. Another writer told me to make the examples as dramatic as possible, so that the hard-core doubters might believe what was being said. Instead, I have included a small sample of in-depth stories similar to what could be found within a woman's circle of acquaintances if she started asking for them. The names of people and places in this book have been changed to protect privacy.

Personal stories are presented to balance the professional explanations provided; my greatest task in writing this book has been to combine the personal experience of birth and healing with the professional responsibility I have taken on by license and education.

Read this book and take strength, comfort, and encouragement to heal yourself. To begin, here is the rock-bottom experience of my first child's birth. As I later came to realize, my experiences weren't as uncommon as I originally thought them to be. Perceptions have changed, healing has occurred, and this story is now a valued part of my personal and family history.

Labor is slow, contractions are now ten minutes apart as they have been for eight hours since I woke up at 5 A.M. Twenty hours have passed since the first contractions began after the movie we went to last night. Michael stays home from work, bustling in the kitchen, washing dishes while I lie on the couch passing time on the phone to friends. Out of the blue Ceci calls. She had her baby, Esther, three weeks early, about six weeks ago.

"I had a strong feeling about you this morning, Lynn. How *are* you doing?"

I describe my labor to her. She says, "It'll get a lot worse before it's over." Not what I want to hear.

Later I move to our bed upstairs. Our labor coach Catherine comes over and massages my feet. A midwife on the phone encourages me to stay home for now. I am still expecting some pain, some excitement, and in a few hours the baby's head will crown out of my vagina and it will be over.

The underground world is most difficult to ignore while in labor as the baby is being born. I am going deeper, and cannot turn back or make the baby stay inside. I could deny being on this journey, but I am on it even in the beginning stages of labor when contractions are irregular and faint.

My sweet dream of going on a journey to a land filled with brilliant-colored flowers, green fields, and sparkling mountains keeps returning to me. I sense spirits, available if I allow them to be.

Then labor begins in earnest with a fireball in my lower back, a knife is wedged between two vertebrae, is being twisted. I hold my breath, and my body is tense. I tell Catherine, "Push on it as hard as you can—no, down a little bit." She rubs the worst spot, reminding me to breathe, relax, let my muscles hang. How can I concentrate on my cervix opening when this back pain inspires me to throw up?

I call the midwife again, she talks to me through a contraction and agrees that labor is intense enough that we can come to the hospital now.

We load up the car and take off with Catherine driving behind us. Michael keeps stopping for so many red lights, and I ask him to please run through them. Each time we stop it seems I'm having a contraction and am thrown forward, and there's no relief from the back pain. I am afraid that the baby is ready to come out right now in the car.

Michael drops me off at the front door where we were instructed to go. An orderly walks up, looks at me and asks Catherine, "Has this woman been shot?" I appear so hysterical to her. Catherine explains "No, she's just in labor," and the orderly puts me in a wheelchair. She runs me up to the fourth floor where the midwife unit is located, Catherine running beside me. The wheelchair is old with a wooden seat, and I feel like a character in a Laurel and Hardy movie. I am deposited in a room facing the cathedral across the street, a stained glass window in the view. The midwife on duty, Joan, checks me as I lay on the double bed, and I'm only two centimeters dilated. Michael hurries into the room with our two bags full of clothes, candles, and baby outfits. I calm down, the contractions slow down; here we are at the hospital. Hurry up and wait.

Labor recalls my origin, my own birth. I have travelled this path before. The way underground is blocked, as though the mud is too thick to fall through. That mass of family history and pain has to be passed through, shoved through, lifted off and away. Any method that would work is fine. Then the birth canal can be travelled; this new little being does not have to be swept away by a repeating pattern. I shove the mud away, and focus on my cervix opening up—that is what is underneath the family pain. Feel it, go for it.

I want to be in the bathtub. It is another reason why we chose these midwives, they provide tubs with bath pillows. We get set up, Michael beside me to press on my back during contractions. A warm washcloth soothes my belly. I am so uncomfortable, and begin hoping someone will ask me if I want pain medication.

Catherine helps me imagine my cervix opening, tells me, "You're doing fine. Focus on your breath, direct it to the center of your cervix, let your pain do its work." That helps, to direct the pain, make it useful. But I still am terrified, am still hoping for medication. Me who hasn't taken an aspirin in five years.

The midwife Joan is concerned because the baby is two weeks late and the labor so long; she wants to hook up a monitor before even considering medication, which I have already asked about. This means I have to get out of the bathtub, which I do not want to do. Besides, *now* she's concerned? I thought I wasn't supposed to be concerned. I flash on the midwife appointment yesterday, when they were all joking with me, saying late babies do just fine. What was going on here? I don't want a monitor. Joan says, "I will just check to make sure the baby's doing fine and then you can get back in the bathtub."

I am on the double bed, straps around my belly. The baby's heart rate is slowing to 50-60 beats during a contraction. Joan calls an obstetrician, Dr. Martin, to consult over the readout. I don't want to be bothered. *I* know there is nothing wrong. This baby will be born through the birth canal, if I'm just given enough time. I'm doing it! I'm doing it! Then I throw up—lying on my back, the liquid arcs and splatters on my chest and face and a nurse cleans me up. Joan hooks up an internal monitor, breaking the bag of waters to do this, and only a few drops of fluid dribble out of me. She is surprised there is no gush, I am dry. One wire goes to the baby's head and the other goes into my uterus. We are both connected to this machine that beeps and lights up. I don't look at it.

This journey underground is much deeper than during the pregnancy. It is exposing my bad dreams, my fears, whatever they are. I am hidden yet exposed as the underground encloses me. The journey is out of my control and I cannot make the fears go away. They demand acceptance as I tumble down the river flowing further underground, gasping for air and fighting the tide. I see pairs of eyes in the darkness, they say, "We are your fears." I get close to naming one of them—it might be death. I plunge into the river and begin to float; then these demon fears are satisfied that I know they are part of me. The journey is eased though still painful.

I throw up two more times. An IV is put in, Joan says because I'm losing so much fluid by throwing up. An oxygen mask is placed over my face to counteract the lowered heart rate during contractions. I lie on my left side, legs curled up. "Take deeper breaths, Lynn." I suck in air as though a life depended on it. My face and hands go numb. I beg for ice. Michael is constantly telling me to breathe, relax; he and Catherine take turns pushing on my lower back to keep the fireball at bay. Occasionally Joan walks away from the beeping machine and puts her face close to mine, saying, "You can find your inner strength, you can do it." I don't feel any better when she does that.

A c-section could end all this misery—ah, a momentary lack of faith as I lie there hooked up, with weak, tense limbs. No, I want to birth this baby through my vagina, *my* way. Oh, God, only dilated another half centimeter. You've got to be kidding! Catherine says, "Let's get you up and moving, you don't have any energy lying there. This is getting tiresome."

Joan went along with the idea, as she was concerned I hadn't peed. The IV had been going for several hours, there was enough fluid in me. "Pee, it would help if you peed, Lynn." People and machines all move to the bathroom. While sitting on the toilet, I'm hooked up at my arm, between my legs, and around my face with tubes, tape, needles, wires. No, I can't pee. I can sit here, my legs shaking, lean forward with my arms around Catherine's waist, and get through this minute by minute. During one contraction the mucous plug passes. A good sign.

Glimpses of my dream flash in me, hidden amongst the back labor. I am shocked that it hurts so much; why didn't my dream warn me? As each wave of pain courses through, I fight, try to conquer, wish it were gone. Oh, but this pain is necessary, useful. This is good pain. It means my cervix can open, can unfold like a flower blossoming. Stand back and let the pain do its work. Breathe into it. Surrender to this pain, just watch it. This is magic. Go deeper

inside. Where death gives way to life. I am already so far under-
ground, where the forces of the earth cannot be denied. Feel the
pulse of the earth as the moon tugs and pulls, shifts her sands,
heaves her waters. Now I flow with the pain, pulse outward and
inward. Flow down the river with the life/death force to an unknown
place, my body drawing strength from the journey. I can feel the tiny
baby in me stirring, doing its own work, travelling its own journey,
both separate and part of me.

Four centimeters. Okay, I'm making progress. I am (happy?)
wanting to make a thumbs up gesture. The midwife and Dr. Martin
continue to fret, still concerned. But I'm doing so well now. So long
as Catherine reminds me every contraction that it's useful pain and
what it's supposed to be doing. So long as they push on my back,
they take away the overwhelming edge of pain so I can birth, focus
on the cervix.

What's that you say, a pH test of the baby's blood? I don't
think it's necessary. They prepare me for the test. I try to ignore the
commotion. One leg is hoisted onto Michael's shoulder, shaking like
a sewing machine needle. Contractions are three minutes apart.
Catherine is pushing on my lower back and reminding me to concentrate on the useful, necessary pain. Someone's got her hands
up my vagina. Dr. Martin is a woman, and is at least six months
pregnant. It hurts. She should know better. She can't get the sac off
the baby's head to get a blood sample, due to the lack of amniotic
fluid and the sac's thickness. An hour goes by in this position. I
dilate to six-plus centimeters and am triumphant! Now I'm really
cooking. See? Even while you fret I'm giving birth. I am slowly loos-
ening up, beginning to understand I have to be relaxed in order for
this baby to move through me.

The sample results come back so acidic the doctor doesn't
believe them and orders another test. My leg is hoisted onto
Michael's shoulder again, as I focus on listening to Catherine's
instructions. I am lost in opening up my cervix, while the rest of the
room is doing something else that involves my body but does not
involve me. I am high on giving birth, and know the baby can soon
move downward. Hooked up to all the machines, hands in me, I
don't care. My life force is strong. The results of the second test are
the same high acidity indicating close to no oxygen in the baby's
blood. I sense confusion and action all around me. One of the nurses runs out of the room after Joan has ordered her to get a gurney.
The doctor is talking to Michael. I won't let in the fear that pulses in
the room. Catherine says in my ear, "Do you understand, Lynn, that
you are going to have a c-section?" I say yes, though still believing

I'm going to give birth my own way, somehow.

Nurses help me onto the gurney, still hooked up everywhere. They're running down the hall. With the IV pole in one hand and her head bobbing beside me, Catherine says, "What are you scared about?"

"I'm scared for me and I'm scared for the baby." Though I don't know my fear. I'm just angry they are interrupting me.

The contractions are continuous now as we arrive in a brightly lit room that contains more equipment than I can imagine. Someone scrapes a dry razor on my pubic hair, leaving me with a goatee. A catheter is crammed up and pints of urine run down. Joan stands beside me saying, "I knew she had to go."

They move me to an operating table. Someone yells, "Lie down!"

"I can't, can't you see I'm pregnant?" A hand helps me down. Someone yells, "Put your legs straight!"

"I can't. I'm having a contraction." Hands jerk my legs straight and they're strapped down. I'm shaking all over. I look up into the anesthetist's eyes and yell, "Put me under before they cut me open." I'm afraid of feeling more pain; especially this scalpel pain that I don't want. They swab my belly, my tired, hardened, sore belly. Michael is asked who he is and told to leave. Catherine is told by Joan to go get a gown on, she can stay because she is a nurse. She comes running back with it half over her head, and holds my strapped down hand. Michael leans down, kisses me, and tells me he loves me. I turn my head and watch him walk out of the room. Then darkness.

I have just run into a brick wall at 30 miles an hour. The pain collapses me.

I yell, "Those fuckers cut me open." I cling to the side of the gurney. There are people talking—I can't listen to their words until the pain stops. I hear I will get morphine but I have to wait, for some ungodly reason. Now! It has to be now or I will rise up and demolish this room as I have been demolished. "Okay Lynn, you're getting morphine now." I float away.

I have died. I am in the bowels of the earth. Stripped down to bare bone and my bones ground up to dust. From destruction new life is conceived, in an unknown form. The journey upward begins here on a new, unfamiliar course. A different river, to an unknown outcome. All I feel is grief, though there is the promise of new life.

"You had a boy, Lynn, and he's fine." Catherine tells me.

"You mean he's not retarded or anything?"

"No, he looks great. He was born three hours ago, he's having a bath now with Michael. Do you want to see him?"

"Not yet, I hurt too much." Catherine says good-by, she is going home to sleep now that I'm awake and the baby is okay. At six in the morning, two nights have gone by since labor began.

Michael comes in and tells me how he waited outside the operating room alone, not knowing how either of us were doing. The midwife Joan rushed out at one point and told him "Lynn is alive," then she rushed back in. Later she burst through the doors with a baby in her arms and said, "We're too busy with your wife, would you take him back to your room?" She put the baby in his arms, and rushed back in to the operating room without another word. In amazement after all that had happened, Michael walked back down the hall alone with his baby. He was able to be with our son from then on, he didn't have to be separated. Michael jokes that Evan had his first men's group already, as the pediatrician who checked him out was also male.

The recovery room nurse bathes me gently, laying warm, wet blankets over me. I'm sticky with blood from birth and from having my belly cut open. My vagina doesn't hurt at all; it's supposed to, but it doesn't. My stomach hurts. No wonder, it's been knifed clean through. This nurse is also pregnant. I wonder how it is for her to see me in my panicked state. When she is finished Michael brings Evan in. I turn my head; he looks pretty good. He looks like an elf with a little white cap on his head. Michael smiles and looks tired.

The journey was interrupted and rerouted. The birth pain, the necessary pain didn't get to be used. It was shoved aside, bull-dozed over. A different pain replaces it—a dull, red-hot scalpel pain. I had a life-saving operation that has its own necessary pain. But a part of me died. The birth canal aches because it was not used. There is no relief. The river washes over me.

I'm clean now, stabilized, sedated. Nurses wheel me back down the hall to the room. There is a baby in a clear bassinet. I am unable to go over and pick him up because of the pain. Instead three women help me off the gurney into bed—the double bed where I was supposed to give birth. Baby Evan is handed to me. He is only six pounds twelve ounces. He probably lost weight this last week inside of me. His hands are peeling, another sign of a late baby. Michael tells me he is twenty and a half inches long, we have a string bean, tall like both of us. Evan nurses while I lay as passively as possible to avoid moving my belly. I learn he almost died. They thought he was brain damaged, with an Apgar score of one, meconium three days old, and a prolapsed umbilical cord. The placenta was in bad shape, not functioning well. Then the miracle, the

Apgar score jumped to eight after five minutes. Of course, I knew he was fine. I wish they had let me continue to give birth my way. I keep the fear at bay.

There is no way of knowing how life will proceed. I am sacrificed in some way, consciously or unconsciously. I surrender, willingly or unwillingly. The earth is where the dead are buried, compost ferments and breaks down. Decay is elemental. Rooted to the underground, waste flows out freely to be recycled—terror, trauma, anger, annihilation, all dive into the ground, are welcomed into the ground. The mystery takes over. Baby Evan wanted to live. His life force was so strong, his little heart continued to beat and he came into this world alive. So I bend toward the light, whatever light I can find, for my own heart also continues to beat.

In those first days of my son's life, I feel no joy. A midwife comes in to talk to me. "I'm very sorry your expectations didn't get met." Expectations! Beyond expectations, I landed on another planet. I am only grateful to be alive because Evan is alive. I know the future holds this child who was born precipitously, and that is good. But the present is horrible. The present still holds tubes and catheters, difficulty walking across the room, and inability to care for my own baby. The midwife asks if I've cried at all. I say I haven't because it hurts too much. She thinks I mean too emotionally painful. I mean too physically painful. I want to cry, but my belly screams out with any sob, so I smother them. Too much pain. Don't touch my stomach!

Every midwife we met with during pregnancy told us that the pain of birth was strong, but mothers would forget about it as soon as the baby was born, the pain would disappear like magic. I hate the midwives.

When Evan is two days old I can walk down the hall, leaning on the IV stand, the nurse carrying the catheter bag. Each step is made slowly and carefully. Two more babies have been born since we arrived. I catch a glimpse of one mother already getting ready to leave, fully dressed and able to sit easily on her bed, changing her baby. I turn my head away, and concentrate once more on moving one foot in front of the other.

As the river flows upward, it cleanses. The new life is slowly built, yet much stronger. The shedding of the past continues with every river bend, old crud sifts to the river bottom, allowing new life to grow. I shed old skin, old feelings, old patterns, as my first look at these new surroundings tells me that life is different.

We leave after being in the hospital five days longer than expected. I can walk to the car, but that will be the greatest effort for the day. We arrive at our house, I cry while walking through each room. How can I take care of an infant and recover, myself? I was supposed to go back to work after four weeks—hah! Two weeks will go by before I can change a diaper without gasping.

A friend Iris gives birth three weeks after I do. She is two weeks early, has an eight-hour labor, not even needing an episiotomy—her birth is all that I had wanted and did not get. Iris is ecstatic, healthy, rosy, loving her experience. We are at opposite ends of some sort of spectrum. I rage over my loss, rage at my physical pain, rage that walking is still difficult while others recover in hours or days. I take comfort in knowing only better things are ahead because it couldn't have been much worse. A sleepless night for me now is nothing—for Iris it is more difficult. She is worried she does not know how to care for her baby. I know that something like feeding Evan is a snap. The fact that he is alive makes everything else so easy. I want to get pregnant again as soon as possible so that I too can have a sore vagina, know what it's like to push a baby out into the world, and heal instantly after a baby has been born.

I tell my story over and over, and keep close those friends who will listen to any detail I want to say, who will nurture me as much as I am able to receive, who understand the darkness, who respect its strength.

While preparing to reemerge out to the above-ground world, I rebuild my strength so that I can again be independent—relatively independent—from the raw life forces underground. I learn to draw from any available harvest in whatever form it takes—from food, shelter, the touch of another. I learn to draw strength from sources and people I once may have shunned. What brings me joy is not merely happiness. Instead joy is being alive in the midst of death, joy in that split second, focused on completely, knowing that sorrow is also present. There is new wealth from understanding how life includes this unseen but felt world. When I gently bubble out of the spring where the underground river emerges above ground, I am transformed.

I care for myself while caring for my baby. I watch him grow, and freely release my joy as his joy is freely expressed. I swaddle myself as he is swaddled. I appreciate my own need for sleep and food, as his needs are so clearly expressed by falling asleep anywhere and crying for food. I feel completely secure when he nestles on my shoulder. And then I realize that all of life is like this—every moment, every person, everywhere I am in relationship with life.

The underground current is sensed when I stop and listen. I no longer dread the journey, or wonder where it will take me next time. My birth, another's birth, a miscarriage, an abortion, my death, another's death. Birth/death of dreams; desires, fears. With my feet firmly planted on the ground, I tap into the mystery.

PART I

ACKNOWLEDGING
THE PAIN

The most common and blatant example of the denial of pain about a traumatic birth is the phrase, "What is important is that your baby is beautiful and healthy. That is what matters. Put what happened behind you." Most mothers can come up with their own variations of this phrase. When a baby has not turned out beautiful or healthy, then the saying becomes, "You can always have another baby. Things always turn out for the best." If something jars or thunks inside while hearing those words, a woman is at the beginning of the journey. She is ready to plunge one layer down, seeking a deeper response to someone's well-meant but hurtful words. She knows something is out of tune; she is in pain emotionally, spiritually, and perhaps still physically.

My first response to her is this: "Your pain matters, it is your guide to healing. Please tell me about your pain—not to cripple yourself, but to know yourself better. Say who you are as clearly as possible, and then we can begin to change things. Then you can begin to heal."

What does healing mean? It means identifying and listening to the messages within a woman's pain, including her feelings. Healing means facing fears of the outcome, however the birth occurred. After an unnecessary cesarean, healing means coming to accept the impact on her soul and body and her baby. To accept the event as part of her life. If the cesarean was necessary, healing includes acknowledging her baby was at risk, due to external or internal factors, whether she knew it at the time or not. Accepting the fact that traumatic things do happen to babies is most heartbreaking. Healing includes seeing the birth in a different way—a woman has allowed her body to be cut open to save her baby's life.

If trauma less easily categorized occurs, such as other medical interventions or disrespectful treatment from family or care providers, healing involves sorting out those events in a similar way and including them as part of her life. Through healing a woman becomes ready to say to the world, This is who I am. This is how I want to be treated. This is what I can give to you. A woman is ready to dig into life with both hands; depression, fear, and anger are no longer major roadblocks, but instead these emotions signal that some aspect of her being requires attention.

Healing means other fears and truths are faced, including growing comfortable with the uncertainty of life, facing the difference between who she thinks she is and who she really is and where she thinks she is and where she actually ends up. Healing means developing the ebullient ability to immerse oneself in a task with complete abandon—the task of raising a child, or finding the place where she belongs most clearly on the earth. She stands tall, she is rooted. She seeks the best treatment possible for self and offspring. If she is mistreated, she objects so strongly that the offender, be it an obstetrician, spouse, friend, large agency, even the president, aware or not of the mistreatment, bends from the objection at least a little, if not all the way. The whole earth shifts toward health as you or I or anyone makes a stand.

DENIAL AND AFFIRMATION OF THE IMPACT OF BIRTH 1

Often a new mother will read in a childbirth text something like this: "You may experience strong emotions postpartum, partly due to the heightened levels of naturally occurring hormones, and partly due to the excitement of your baby's birth." Excuse me? I want to sing to the skies and the earth from the bottom of my soul, or, I feel like my heart has been torn in two, and I have no idea where to go from here—and that is how it is described?

To affirm birth in any form, its power and life-giving force for all involved, requires acknowledgement of all kinds of impact—positive and negative, loving and hateful, painful and pleasant. Emotions experienced in any birth are strong. Instead of bursting through the roof, they may be swallowed. For some, a lifelong appreciation of birth quietly percolates in a woman's private self. For others an important part of the self is cut off; that attempt to sever or bury or distance a piece of the self is denial.

Interwoven into culture and personal histories is a lack of awareness of the impact of birth. Often learned from society and family, this denial can destroy any one person. For example, the uncertainty of birth is rarely discussed. To acknowledge the possibility of anything less than a healthy baby and mother is taboo, and one's own fear of an unexpected outcome understandably feeds denial. Yet when the darker side of birth is acknowledged, a wealth of tools becomes available. These tools can help anyone cope with what is inside oneself and with the external world.

Instead of dealing with uncertainty as a natural part of life, unexpected birth events are often treated as catastrophes or freak occurrences. This approach feeds fear instead of trust and acceptance. Additionally, anything short of a catastrophe is discounted, and there is little opportunity to embrace birth as it happens. This attitude prevails both for reproductive losses and for traumatic births.

Unexpected outcomes and interventions happen frequently. For example, miscarriage rates are between 20 and 25 percent of known conceptions; stillbirth rates are 1 percent, and neonatal deaths occur at a rate of 1 percent. Overall in the United States, these add up to one million birth-related losses per year. Though not the focus of this book, these losses do impact subsequent pregnancies and births, contributing to later traumas, as outlined in chapters 4 and 8.

The cesarean rate in the United States in 1990 was 22.7 percent. The episiotomy rate in many hospitals is 90 percent; the rate of epidurals used during labor can be as high as 80 percent. These interventions, among many others, are not always unnecessary or unwanted. They do, however, indicate a high degree of trauma, both physical and emotional.

DENIAL OF PAST HISTORY

How a woman was born and how she lives her life have great impact on how she will give birth. In order to understand these connections, information from her mother or from deep within herself will have to be sought. This information can be another layer of denial to identify and reconcile. Birth history is easy to discount, because a woman often hears, "What difference does it make? You've lived your whole life since then; it couldn't have been such a big deal—you were born alive, weren't you? That's all you need to know. Why, I know of someone who was so small, he spent his first six weeks in a shoe box next to the wood stove. . . "

How a woman lives her life and prepares for the birth has a significant connection to birth. Denial makes it easier to say after some labor or birth difficulty, "Who knows why these things happen? You can't always prepare." The outcome of labor is not completely random. When something unplanned happens, the important point is not to assign blame or to judge, but to become aware of the power within oneself to *influence* the natural process of birth, or the natural process of healing after a traumatic birth. This topic is covered in more depth in chapter 4.

The influence of a woman's life on the birth of her baby implies the presence of power within her. Denial of her ability to influence means denial of her inner power.

The aftershocks of birth create far-reaching changes for everyone involved. During my first pregnancy, I minimized the upcoming changes, expecting that life would go on primarily as before the baby arrived, with a few accommodations. I planned a four-week maternity leave, expecting then to go back to work full-time. This insulating stance allowed me to get through a difficult pregnancy. Already over-whelmed, I didn't want to know how difficult the task would be. If I'd admitted the difficulty, I wouldn't consciously have made the commit-ment to become pregnant. My friend Linda said once, "If parents told prospective parents the truth about what raising kids is like, the race would become extinct." I said to myself many times during that first pregnancy, "I'm sure I'll be able to manage with a new baby. It will be different for me." This denial serves a purpose—actually all denial does, the purpose of insulating us from how deep our feelings are, how monumental a situation is.

Minimizing the upcoming changes her baby will make in a wom-an's life is not always a major component of a traumatic birth. However, minimizing upcoming changes can contribute to a difficult labor. Unconsciously a woman might not want the baby to arrive. Maybe she wishes she hadn't ever gotten pregnant, or perhaps she and her partner just had a fight, and this new baby's life is not wholly wel-come. She may not have a partner and may not know how to cope. Or she may be a perfectionist and want this baby to wait because she hasn't decorated the baby's room yet. To relax and open herself to a baby entering the world through her body is not what she wants to do. If birth trauma does occur, those unrealistic expectations of so little change contribute to overload her already stressed psyche and body.

Birth is often framed as the addition of a baby to a family; no room is made for loss, though loss is more of a guarantee than the gains involved. Loss is part of any change, and certainly part of birth. A woman says good-by to her old child-free life, to her body as it was before pregnancy, and then to the pregnancy after the birth.

During my first pregnancy the birth class we attended only scratched the surface of this issue. Looking back, the instructor was informative yet not thorough. Would we have been shocked if she gave feedback about her perceptions of which of us would have a difficult labor? I recall telling her my plans of a four-week maternity leave; she replied, "That might be a tough thing to do." I could have used a birth educator sitting me down for at least six individual classes to serious-ly discuss my expectations about labor and having a baby. Taking a different class may also have helped, for some birth educators do a more thorough job than I experienced. After the class ended I thought, "Oh well, I have no idea what's going to happen, and I paid attention in class, so I'm going to trust that my body will know what to do when it's time to do it." I left the class ignoring my fear and total incomprehension of the purpose of labor pain, as well as of what life would be like with a new baby. I was tight as a clam, my body so tense my legs ached. Denial was alive and well, though my body spoke volumes of truth.

Michael later confirmed that he believed his job during labor was to tell me that everything would be okay. He had not been prepared to support the existence of fear and pain. Instead, the best simulation of labor this class provided was when Michael pinched my hand so I could practice breathing through a contraction. It wasn't until the birth of our second baby that he recognized the value of acknowledging and embracing fear and pain, and this task was not easy for him.

Denial about not feeling ready for change eats at a woman. She keeps it inside, because it is not socially or personally acceptable to say, "I don't want this baby now, maybe I've made a huge mistake. I can't pull it off. What have I done? My life is about to end, maybe I'll die in labor." If she expresses these fears and her disgust with the situation to someone supportive, the energy released will move her to where she needs to go next. Holding on to any feeling manifests in constriction, the opposite of opening herself to birth.

DENIAL BETWEEN PARTNERS

After the birth, many couples have rifts that become chasms as birth trauma issues remain silent between them. One couple came to see me two years after an unnecessary cesarean following a failed induction. There was no indication the baby was endangered, no apparent reason for a cesarean other than to have the birth happen that very day. The woman, Judy, had a history of late babies, no complications, and mild labors. After the pitocin failed to induce contractions, Judy wanted to go home. Her husband Roger wanted to do what the doctor said, which was to go ahead with a cesarean. Judy was pressured by them both to sign consent forms and deliver cesarean. She was angry in a rock-hard way, and could not trust Roger afterwards. She blamed him for causing the cesarean and for not listening to her about what she believed her body was capable of.

Not only did Judy have the cesarean trauma to heal, but her relationship with Roger was wounded as well. She said she'd been looking over her shoulder ever since, not able to trust that her body would not be sabotaged by Roger again. Until this couple saw me, they had not discussed the issue at all. Their daily lives were filled with daily details. They unconsciously denied that a problem existed and originally came to see me for unrelated issues: money and an upcoming career change for Roger. Eventually the birth events were uncovered, and they slowly felt secure enough in my office to put a few cards out on the table. Roger poured out his willingness to do anything to prove his trustworthiness to Judy, though it would be a long time before she felt able to take the risk of trusting. Judy, after two years, still had denial that the cesarean had happened at all; she still wished that something could erase its existence, that some miracle could take away her scar, and that she could birth their daughter again. Their iceberg of rage, fear, mistrust, regret, and other powerful issues began to break up, and they slowly built new trust in each other. Denial is powerful, and when it can no longer mask the pain, an unexpected eruption of some sort happens. At that point, some people may drink, use other medicating substances, or enclose themselves in silence in an effort to keep the pain buried. I am always supportive when someone mines the veins of pain instead; healing happens when the festering wound is finally cleansed.

My own iceberg began to break up when my first baby was two months old. At this time, denial about the cesarean was not the issue; I knew full well my unhappiness and disappointment. My husband Michael and I were walking on eggshells, avoiding the conflicts between us that had festered with the stresses of birth and baby. This first eruption of anger between me and Michael illuminates how my own attitudes toward pregnancy and motherhood contributed to post-partum and marital stress.

> Anger suddenly erupted about working each day of my pregnancy. Photos of when I was pregnant showed dark craters under my eyes, an overall worn-out appearance like a ten-year old bath towel, and I hadn't seen that! I was so angry about agreeing to return to work ridiculously early, of agreeing to this superwoman contract that was destroying me. The homemaker and the business-woman—the mother and father—were in violent conflict. *I am a volcano erupting. The lava pours out of me, warming me.*
>
> I buried this anger up until now for the sake of maintaining my career and the tentative stability in our home. Now a new identity demanded a place.
>
> Even though I wanted more than anything to be with my son Evan, my life up until now was built on the premise that I would work and be a success and prove my history wrong that children are a burden and stop you from doing what you want. My work was the most life-giving thing until Evan; I saw no way to do both. The thought of cutting down to part-time felt essential, but it meant betraying my whole former life. To have had the whole first year just

to be with Evan would have been humane, but I couldn't give that opportunity to myself even if it were possible.

"The only thing you know for certain when you're born is you're going to die one of these days." My father had repeated this phrase all my young life, when we told him I was pregnant, and since Evan was born. *If I don't work, if I don't run to my work, then I will die. In so many ways I will die, he told me so. I will lose myself in my children. In the act of giving birth my child will be doomed to death. Where is life? The underground journey was so different from this. The journey that began with Evan's birth showed me life. Where is that path, I can't see it, am too afraid. I cling to work, and cannot change and work less, lose the only escape from death I've had all my life until now.*

But I have to. I face my father and say, "No more will you rule me. I am in the world on my own terms."

Even if changing meant losing our house or a divorce, making this choice felt safe. I looked at Evan in my arms, and his face already told me so much about life. Every cell in his body was precious. We were a family. I turned to look at Michael.

I had lied to myself and to him about being able to work beyond full-time and make a baby at the same time. I thought any amount of stress could be managed. I was strong, tough—tough as they come. Where *was* my husband in this picture? My lover of sixteen years, the father of my child? He was there in the morning fixing me tea as I dragged myself out of bed to get ready for the day, he cooked and cleaned. I did not listen to his challenges or offers of help. He agreed when we were pregnant that he would take care of our baby when I returned to work. I thought that was asking for a lot from a husband. I didn't tell him of my fear of being vulnerable, dependent, and of trusting someone else.

I had lied about being so understanding when Michael lost his business, agreeing to be supportive, both emotionally and financially. Now I was breaking my promise, mad that he had ever started that business, mad that there was no money, and too threatened to let him know that I felt threatened.

The volcano spurts out even more lava, as the father is not obeyed. "I will not work full-time and leave Evan! I am so fucking mad." I yelled.

"What are you talking about? You know I support your staying with him. I'm doing what I can to work more."

"No, you don't get it!" I shouted, "I hate you! I wish you were dead!" Read my lips, I will not work ever again at my old pace. "I will only work as much as it takes to eat. Do you hear me? I don't care beyond that. If you want to keep the house payments going, you're going to have to make the money. I would just as soon live in an apartment." I was triumphant, willing to lose the house if necessary, facing what I thought was the worst that could happen.

"Put Evan down if you're going to yell."

"Fine, I'll put him in his crib." I went into the other bedroom, and laid him down, where he seemed to be okay. I thought he was okay in my arms, as I felt safe, able to make him secure.

I left the house and took a walk around a nearby lake by myself with more energy than in the past year. The day was cold and blustery, early June. I wore the same grey corduroy coat as during pregnancy, now barely keeping me warm, the collar wrapped tightly around my neck. The wind blew on the lake, blew in my face, and I had all the strength needed to walk into it, while crying into worn tissues. Each word of anger had loosened me up. I was free, and would not take back one word. My heart said, "Now I can love."

Michael faced me when I got home. "You hurt me with all those things you said."

I laughed. "What you see is what I am. That's as bad as it gets. I can't be much more angry." We faced each other across the dining room table, the air was tense.

"I don't trust you, those words were meant to hurt me." Michael looked at me directly.

"Fine, you don't like it, but I trust myself. You're just going to have to take it on faith."

"I want you to knock it off, control yourself better."

"If you got scared, okay. But that's all I'm going to hurt you. I'm sorry. I feel better about myself and better about you than I ever have. I know, I could have said this sooner, or maybe a little calmer."

"All right, you said you're sorry. But it'll take a while to trust you. And another thing, don't hold Evan if you're going to yell like that."

"Okay, but I'm not going to keep my mouth shut when I need to fight, it's too essential." And I walked into the kitchen feeling my strength, ready to cook real nourishment for the first time in years.

PHYSICAL REALITIES OF BIRTH

In the overt, concrete world, denial of the physical aspects of birth exists. For example, many women don't realize as they go into labor that they soon may be defecating on the bed or table or floor while pushing out a baby. That's denial in the simplest sense. Then afterwards, many women add to their mortification by not mentioning how embarrassed they were that the defecating happened. Birth is messy. I'm not advocating that television sitcoms include real-life labor scenes, but I do advocate talking about birth more realistically in most every other format.

After my first son's birth I experienced relief when the physical details of a cesarean operation were spelled out. I found an excerpt written by a physician in *Silent Knife* by Nancy Cohen and Lois Estner, precisely describing the operation. Later, my first labor coach Catherine, who was in the operating room with me, gave a very explicit description of the operation and Evan's resuscitation. Those physical descriptions rooted me in reality; my fantasies were sometimes worse than the events themselves. My denial, the kind that wished none of this had ever happened, lessened. Afterwards it was easier to acknowledge the facts: "Yes, I did have a cesarean; here is the scar, and this is how it happened."

Birth is so full of change. This new being is created from the rawest of physical materials, and enters the world to be separate and breathe air for the first time. A woman's own life is forever disrupted, impacted, and sometimes filled with love because of this baby. The rest of her world—work, family, house, neighborhood, everything—is going to shift to include this new person and new parent. Any pregnancy and birth in any form have this power. How could all this change happen without pain? If a woman thought her life was going to continue as it was, only enhanced by this new addition, she experiences grief that it is not so. The physical pain of birth is a concrete reminder about the passage she is traversing. It is a natural consequence of such a relatively huge organic creature leaving her body through an opening which is always present, but only completely open during birth.

If a traumatic birth has occurred and the baby dies, the two issues overlap, and need to be separated. One issue is the grief over her baby dying; the other is about the traumatic birth experience. Death's grief and healing process extend beyond this book's context. A baby or fetus, no matter how long he or she is alive, impacts the rest of one's life on all levels: physical, emotional, and spiritual. Memories emerge bidden or not. If both losses have occurred, it is helpful to recognize the impact they each hold. Grief will be aided by this definition.

One of the worst bills of goods sold is the goal of a pain-free birth. It creates a denial difficult to cut through; who wants to be in physical pain, let alone emotional pain? Birth's pain exists for a reason, and is a gift. The pain is about a woman's body stretching and opening enough for a baby to come through, and then her body pushing the baby out through the vagina, at that moment called the birth canal. A woman's mind and psyche must also stretch and open enough for a baby to come through. How can this happen without some kind of transformation? A cervix opening to ten centimeters in diameter is stuff that science fiction novels are made of. We are so distant from our nature—what seems alien and not of our self needs to be wondrous. The reproductive cycle is a woman's most easily accessible way to cross the barrier into full-fledged personhood. A path of enlightenment often requires a physical ordeal.

When my first baby was born, that pain dropped me underground unwillingly and unhappily, to a whole different world. I was initiated, and later grew appreciative. Every birth story I hear has this potential for transformation. Embracing the pain of labor means a woman will go to an unknown destination. For example, my neighbor birthed her second baby unaided because the baby came out so fast the doctor couldn't get there in time to perform an episiotomy or intervene otherwise. Her daughter slipped right out and my neighbor glowed, literally glowed from this experience for days afterwards.

Our society encourages denial of the purpose of labor pain, as well as denial of any pain. We are encouraged to medicate with a wide variety of substances for physical pain, while emotional pain is either medicated or disregarded completely. When a woman wants to acknowledge pain or view it positively, she stems a strong tide of denial. Also, acknowledging current pain may unleash past personal wounds formerly suppressed and now accessible. She fights uncountable messages to avoid, medicate, and eradicate pain instead.

Intellectual understanding of the dynamics of pain and challenge in birth can exist with little regard for emotional comprehension. In other words, a woman's head can understand, but her gut feelings remain unacknowledged.

She avoids the depth and impact of her birth experience, avoids what her body is trying to tell her. Fear of strong emotions is a primary cause of denial.

Some women have labors so minimal they hardly know it is happening. They have a different kind of birth, no better or worse, just different. A continuum of pain exists in labor, from barely knowing labor is happening to the most painful experience of a woman's life. Pain may also be confused with intensity. All resulting births can be beautiful.

I am not a medical practitioner. The judicious use of painkillers is discussed elsewhere in references on various birth education approaches. I am not radically against medication, and am aware that all I talk about involves personal choice. However, for many women who end up with unnecessary cesareans and unwanted interventions, their labors turned on that path away from natural birth beginning with pain meds. Risks of medication and consequences of denial need to be balanced with the benefits of distance from pain and feelings. If there is potent resistance to pain resulting in tightness, then the numbness provided by medication may serve a valuable purpose, allowing relaxation and decreased panic. The decision is best made when a laboring mother is consulted, when she assesses her own limitations, understands the full range of options, and makes a decision based on what she believes will work for her.

Denial is powerful and seductive because it is about avoiding pain or discomfort. "Let me take away your pain." It is a wily beast, and wreaks havoc afterwards, when the bills come due—when a woman has such emotional pain from lost dreams, betrayals, and violations of her body that she is driven either toward more denial or toward seeking health and releasing the pain.

PREGNANT BODY IMAGE

A woman's physical body obviously goes through changes in pregnancy and birth. She lives in an elephantine form in later pregnancy, and after birth can feel like a stuffed version of her former self. Movements are restricted, and open season exists for comments and unwanted touch from others. If a woman starts out uncomfortable about her body, if any attention drawn to her body is excruciating, then pregnancy will heighten her discomfort because of so much positive and negative attention. During my first pregnancy, at about seven months, while in a store, a woman came up to me and exclaimed, "Oh! You're going to have a baby," and put her hand on my belly. I told her to take her hands off me, and, though I was assertive, it took me a few hours to recover my equilibrium.

Questions like "How much weight have you gained?" "Wow, you look big—are you expecting twins?" "How do you fit in your car?" are not uncommon, and they feed a negative body image. Positive comments such as "You look so beautiful when you're pregnant" and "I love a big belly at the end of pregnancy" are often too few, or not believed when received. Once a positive, loving body image is nurtured, then such comments are sought and believed to be deserved. A negative body image repels affirmations.

The most important aspect of body image is that it is fluid and flexible, and not about how a body looks. The same body can have an extremely positive or negative body image, sometimes within the space of a day. I may feel twenty pounds heavier than I am, and how I feel about my body is much more important than how much I actually weigh.

Negative body image is often a result of past abuse—emotional, physical, or sexual. To avoid one's negative body image, coping mechanisms frequently employed are to maintain the sensation of living only from the neck up or to remain completely out of one's body. Both are versions of denial. Attempts to stay out of one's body in a dissociated state are coping mechanisms used to avoid the impact of abuse.

Damage can be caused more subtly than by outright abuse. For example, an individual could be told as a small child, "You have such skinny ankles, just like your grandma. They're like bird legs," or "If only you weren't so big, you could still ride on your daddy's shoulders." If reinforced with similar comments, and never or rarely eclipsed by affirmative statements, these words will blossom into a sense of physical inadequacy, either of being too much or too little. Though more subtle, the impact is often potent, resulting in the same drive to dissociate from or berate one's body.

In contrast, a child who grows up appreciating what her body is capable of doing and how beautiful she is just because of her existence, a child who is not compared with others, will feel confidence and strength.

Pregnancy requires a rootedness in the physical body. This makes it imperative for a woman to enter her body, acknowledge its pain and strength, and allow it to do the work and creation of baby making. Pregnancy can be a powerful opportunity for healing body image. Without healing, pregnancy can be a powerful force for a woman to further separate from her body or to further deny abuse, putting her at risk for perpetuating the same abuse and an even worse body image. Body image is a powerful component of birth. If a woman integrates herself so that she can be in and appreciate her body and use its power, she will participate in an empowering birth experience.

I have the utmost compassion for women struggling with body image, and know the pain of someone drawing attention to skinny or fat ankles, large or small breasts, or a protruding stomach. Knowing how exposed she will be during delivery can trigger dissociation from her body and add to a woman's lack of preparation for the upcoming event. Exposure can trigger shame and tension, the opposite emotions needed for a positive birth.

The desire to separate from her body promotes avoidance of pain and can lead to increased interventions. If trauma occurs, the negative body image that follows may prohibit a woman from telling others what happened to her, further promoting shame and a desire to separate from her body.

Acceptance and appreciation for one's body helps it heal. A woman with a positive body image is more than halfway toward a healthy, normal birth. She embraces her body's power and ability to birth a baby, appreciates how miraculous body functions are, and the birth connects her with her body like nothing else. After trauma, a positive body image enables a woman to better appreciate her body's potential and ability to heal, and its power to fight back as needed throughout recovery.

During my second full-term pregnancy I was talking to my nurse friend Catherine about the miraculous body changes happening, how a baby is made out of basic elements, and I was carrying around a miracle growing in my womb. I was lit from within. She interrupted, saying, "Lynn, birth isn't a miracle. If there were no sperm involved with making a baby, that would be a miracle." I laughed. Catherine always brings me back down to earth in my musings. This exchange reflects enjoyment of my body, the pleasure of being pregnant, and ability to absorb teasing without falling apart—the antithesis of a negative body image.

During this second pregnancy I put body affirmations on the refrigerator door, reminding me to love my body, to enjoy food, exercise, and the shape of my belly, and to anticipate a wonderful, relaxed birth. All of those affirmations worked.

A woman's body is transformed in pregnancy, and like her life it will have permanently changed. The same body image issues she had before will manifest with the focus on resultant changes, exacerbated by more denial of pain or trauma. This transformation is more painful when there is trouble acknowledging womanhood. Large breasts filled with milk for a nursing baby, the round stomach of a new mother, and the general softening of her appearance are all symbols of the potential of her new life as a mother. These symbols are in conflict with many images of a "successful" woman. The unrealistic, harmful expectations and stereotypes of a woman as thin, young, and curvaceously sexy are not met. If taken seriously, this can mean her body is to be hidden and unacknowledged.

With a cesarean birth, a scar must also be reckoned with, a permanent piece of evidence that the body was cut open for the baby to be born. An episiotomy scar, though more hidden, holds the same power and often is in need of affirmation and acceptance. Scars can be seen as evidence of the body's failure to perform rather than the miracle of a healed wound. At first I hated my cesarean scar and wanted it to disappear.

My scar repulsed me, if possible I would have obliterated it. Touching and rubbing healing oils into the scar helped, then I knew my child entered the world through my stomach. As a child, I believed that babies came out through a woman's belly button; I recalled going to a wedding with my parents at age five. *I am standing on the pew to see, and while watching the ceremony I figure out all on my own that when two people get married, God zaps them so that they will have a child. I have no concept that the baby comes out from between a woman's legs, thinking either it will come out like a ghost walking through a wall, or the belly button will open up to let the baby out.*

Did that belief guide Evan out through my stomach?

The terror of being cut open was still with me. I was living proof that we draw to ourselves what we are most afraid of. During pregnancy, while reading countless books on the subject, I always avoided the chapters on cesareans or infant loss. It was extremely unlikely that that kind of birth would happen—a prolapsed cord or placenta previa occurred less than 1 percent of the time, so I wouldn't even consider the possibility. Determined to give birth vaginally, even in the operating room I tried to defy the surgeon. But they strapped me down and cut me open no matter what I wanted.

Every fear, every humiliation, every agony is swallowed. I never open my mouth. Never, never. But the underground journey insists on respect of fear, insists on an open mouth that bays at the moon, insists on accepting life in any form. The incision in the belly was an initiation, not the end like I want to think.

Scars had always meant evil to me. A scar-faced man in a book meant a gangster, or a knife fight, or some horrid, deforming accident that caused a person to wear a mask forever, and people would faint at the unmasked sight. A scarred woman was always hidden, women don't have scars.

My scar was red and upraised, knotted and lumpy, looked angry and very imperfect. I hated it, seeing only failure. My body would never be the same.

Right before the drugs took effect, I had pictured the surgeon brandishing the evil knife, its blade glinting in the bright light. She stood sinister above my belly, relishing the first cut, as though she did it for fun. I owed her an apology.

When Evan was five months old I was confronted by a healer who said, "Why *are* you hanging on to your anger? So what if you're not perfect? You're healthy, I can't find anything wrong with you. Your son is healthy and was born how and when he needed to be born. It's wonderful you played that part in his life."

Health did not mean being perfect, love did not mean never failing. My body was whole, my son was whole. Health meant being alive.

That same healer said, "What if your scar were your child who was mistreated or was born deformed, how would you treat it then?" Oh, if it were my child, I would want to give comfort and nourishment. Her question made sense—the scar was like an ugly, deformed child that was part of me. I could love any child—I could love myself. I gently rubbed in healing oils, massaging the adhesions.

The scar was my war wound, and I began to look at it with pride, seeing more clearly the miracle of a gaping wound healing, and the wonder of a live baby.

The only way I know to manifest a true body change in shape or power or perception is to affirm and love one's body as it presently is. Kindness and acceptance promote growth toward health. Acknowledgment of the body's hard work and efforts to cooperate with our wishes and needs goes far in building a relationship to the body in which one lives.

After my first birth, I could find few places to share what happened to me and be listened to without people denying how traumatic the experience had been. I was also afraid of exposing to others what I considered huge personal mistakes and shortcomings: not being able to birth vaginally, miscalculating my ability to work full-time as a new mother, and feeling my scar's presence as punishment. As I slowly began telling my story to certain women, they reciprocated with their stories, and I was no longer alone, no longer in a void or holding pattern. My story is included and made accessible to other women in an effort to provide a bridge and tool. I am here to say to every woman: your journey and story matter, they are guiding forces in your life wanting to be heard. Please listen, and tell your story.

FOR WORK ON YOUR OWN

I advocate all forms of self-expression. Writing, painting, talking, singing, dancing, any type of outpouring can help loosen up whatever is inside. After reading this short piece, there may be rumblings of grief, anger, or fear from your own experiences and fear of what you may find. At the end of each chapter several questions are included to use as a starting point to navigate your own healing. They are answerable with any format. You may just wish to meditate on them. Keep a journal, which can be the beginning of your own story telling. Create a notebook of drawings charting your course. Make sounds of any nature, guttural voicings that need expression from current or past grief about the birth. Cry. Stamp your feet. Sing a lullaby over and over. Make up a tune with the words *baby, softness, in the night.* Sing a song you already know that would give you comfort. Do you like to move? One woman read one of these chapters each day, then went out for her daily run. This was her way of incorporating what she was learning. She pounded out her anger and let her mind roam freely.

Question One: What do I do when I am told something I don't want to hear? How do I close myself off from uncomfortable information? How do I open myself to hear uncomfortable information?

Question Two: How have I been told to ignore my baby's birth experience? What have others said that have kept my words deep in my throat? If I let the words out, what would they be? If I let out the first word about the birth of my baby, what would it be? Each time a story is told, denial is chipped down, like a flake of wood chiseled from a piece of sculpture. The first word is the beginning of the sculpture.

Question Three: How am I aware that my birth experience may be more important than I have yet acknowledged?

FOR FURTHER READING

A complete reference section is at the end of the book. Specific texts that expand or substantiate the content of each chapter are listed at its end for easy access.

Infant Loss

Ilse, Sherokee. (1982) *Empty Arms: A Guide to Help Parents and Loved Ones Cope with Miscarriage, Stillbirth, and Neonatal Death.* Minneapolis, MN: Wintergreen Press.

Ilse, Sherokee, and Burns, Linda Hammer. (1985) *Miscarriage: A Shattered Dream.* Minneapolis, MN: Wintergreen Press.

Panuthos, Claudia, and Romeo, Catherine. (1984) *Ended Beginnings: Healing Childbearing Losses.* New York: Warner Books.

Body Image

Borysenko, Joan. (1987) *Minding the Body, Mending the Mind.* New
    York: Bantam.
___. (1990) *Guilt Is the Teacher, Love Is the Lesson.* New York: Warner.
Chernin, Kim. (1982) *The Obsession: Reflections on the Tyranny of
    Slenderness.* New York: Harper Colophon.
Freeman, Rita. (1988). *Bodylove.* New York: Harper & Row.
Hutchinson, Marcia. (1985) *Transforming Body Image.* Trumansburg,
    NY: The Crossing Press.
Wolf, Naomi. (1991) *The Beauty Myth: How Images of Beauty Are Used
    against Women.* New York: Morrow.

Mythological, Philosophical, and Historical Birth References

Arms, Suzanne. (1975) *Immaculate Deception.* Boston: Houghton
    Mifflin.
Capra, Fritjof. (1982) *The Turning Point: Science, Society, and the
    Rising Culture.* Simon & Schuster.
Davis-Floyd, Robbie. (1992) *Birth as an American Rite of Passage.*
    Berkeley: University of California Press.
Mitford, Jessica. (1992) *The American Way of Birth.* New York:
    Dutton.

General Information about Cesareans

Peterson, Gayle, and Mehl, Louis. (1985) *Cesarean Birth: Risk and
    Culture.* Berkeley, CA: Mindbody.
VanTuinen, Ingrid, and Wolfe, Sidney. (1992) *Unnecessary Cesarean
    Sections: Halting a National Epidemic.* Washington, D.C.:
    Public Citizen's Research Group.

TRAUMA: CESAREANS AND MAJOR INTERVENTIONS

2

Trauma is defined by Webster's Dictionary as: "1a: an injury (as a wound) to living tissue caused by an extrinsic agent <surgical~> b: a disordered psychic or behavioral state resulting from mental or emotional stress or physical injury 2: an agent, force, or mechanism that causes trauma." Based on this and other definitions, each mother can decide if how she gave birth was traumatic or not. She can create her own definition. One essential guideline is that if she feels traumatized, she was. Filling in the details may come later. Remember this during the postpartum checkup, when the doctor or nurse, do not acknowledge the trauma of the loss of a vaginal birth or the use of other interventions. Sometimes no reference to these events is made, or perhaps one's own acknowledgment of trauma is discounted.

A psychological/medical model of trauma provides further elucidation. This information helps counteract self-doubt and denying attitudes that many births are normal, natural, and nothing to be upset about, when the mother is indeed upset. Several birth stories are related throughout the book as examples. They include a necessary cesarean, an unnecessary cesarean, and the major use of other interventions. The described births are actually points on a continuum; if an individual cannot specifically relate to one story, her birth experience is on a different location on the continuum. Even without major intervention, minor trauma follows a similar pattern. For example, if a woman's separation from her baby immediately after birth for the first hours is traumatic; healing is necessary and valuable. In this case, the wound can be fears of not knowing who and where her baby is, loss of those first hours of bonding, and a lasting foreboding that her baby will disappear.

Are all births traumatic? My assumption is no, some are not.

Some births are healthy and normal, and leave a woman feeling peaceful, powerful, and hopeful. A few stitches, a sore body, or fears and tears about new responsibilities are not necessarily the traumas that require the kind of healing I describe. My second full-term pregnancy ended in a hospital birth that left me feeling totally satisfied. Afterwards, it was so easy to recover that I almost looked for something to be panicked or upset about. Any birth requires great effort and immense change physically, emotionally, and spiritually. Those issues are healthy and normal, and will be in a woman's life throughout the birthing process and beyond.

Now I am putting on my professional hat, with my mother hat peeking out from underneath. From a psychological perspective, birth trauma can result in posttraumatic stress disorder (PTSD), a diagnosis listed in the Diagnostic and Statistical Manual (DSM-III-R) written by the American Psychiatric Association. Most mental health practitioners refer to the DSM-III-R for diagnoses and help in conceptualizing a treatment plan. These diagnoses are also required for insurance claims. If a woman sees a therapist for healing or for relief from distress, she might be given the diagnosis of PTSD. Other diagnoses may be used as well, including adjustment reaction, generalized anxiety disorder, and dysthymia.

Within the medical profession and its influential sphere, this diagnosis of PTSD needs to be more frequently related to traumatic births. Learning this information and rejecting or embracing the concept is a way to educate and validate oneself, no matter what other professional authorities say.

In the following section, I delineate the DSM-III-R description of post-traumatic stress disorder and relate specific symptoms to birth experiences. I use my own trauma response as an example to highlight the diagnosis. Later, other women's stories elucidate this diagnosis. The following description can be referred to whenever there is confusion or doubt that trauma occurred.

Here is the DSM-III-R (pp. 247-251) description and my narrative:

> A. The person has experienced an event that is outside the range of usual human experience and that would be markedly distressing to almost anyone, e.g., serious threat to one's life or physical integrity; serious threat or harm to one's children, spouse, or other close relatives and friends; sudden destruction of one's home or community; or seeing another person who has recently been or is being, seriously injured or killed as the result of an accident or physical violence.

The birth of my first son fits this criteria: it was beyond the range of usual human experience and markedly distressing, my baby's life was seriously threatened, my own physical integrity was threatened, and the disruption to our lives felt catastrophic. Note that if a woman believes that her baby's life is threatened, even if it actually isn't, she would be traumatized also. A doctor's threat that if she does not follow his or her orders then the baby might die puts a woman in a terribly compromised position. This reaction is often experienced with unnecessary cesareans; the baby is born hale and healthy with no apparent cause for distress. Note that if the partner witnesses a traumatic birth, he or she also has a road of recovery to travel. Also note that a woman giving birth to a baby that needs immediate and aggressive medical care experiences trauma separate from the birth trauma.

The DSM-III-R continues the description as follows:

> B. The traumatic event is persistently reexperienced in at least one of the following ways:
>
> (1) recurrent and intrusive distressing recollections of the event
> (2) recurrent distressing dreams of the event
> (3) sudden acting or feeling as if the traumatic event were recurring (includes a sense of reliving the experience, illusions, hallucinations, and dissociative [flashback] episodes, even those that occur upon awakening or when intoxicated)
> (4) intense psychological distress at exposure to events that symbolize or resemble an aspect of the traumatic event, including anniversaries of the trauma.

After Evan's birth, I had all four symptoms: (1) I could not get the birth out of my mind, recalling the hallway walls and lights as the gurney was being pushed by running nurses, and I recalled the feeling of being prepped for surgery, among many other recollections; (2) my dreams were often visited by anxieties about my son's well-being, particularly intense fears of him not being resuscitated in time; (3) I had flashbacks of the sensation of waking in the recovery room—the clang of the bed rail as I clung to it, the effort of trying to climb into the regular bed while my body was racked with pain—and I had uncountable flashbacks of each memory of the birth; (4) I had intense psychological distress whenever anyone else talked about her birth, positive or negative, trauma-filled or not. Any birth reminded me of Evan's birth, and I would dissociate on the spot. On the first anniversary, Evan's first birthday, I had a strong visceral and mental memory of his birth. I want to say immediately that these responses are not only symptoms of a problem. They were all, because I paid attention to them, ways I cleared out the trauma. They were part of the healing process. Trouble is caused when these responses are ignored or denied.

The DSM-III-R further defines PTSD in the following way:

> C. Persistent avoidance of stimuli associated with the trauma or numbing of general responsiveness (not present before the trauma) as indicated by at least three of the following:
>
> (1) efforts to avoid thoughts or feelings associated with the trauma
> (2) efforts to avoid activities or situations that arouse recollections of the trauma
> (3) inability to recall an important aspect of the trauma (psychogenic amnesia)
> (4) markedly diminished interest in significant activities
> (5) feeling of detachment or estrangement from others
> (6) restricted range of affect, e.g., unable to have loving feelings
> (7) sense of a foreshortened future, e.g., does not expect to have a career, marriage, or children, or a long life

I believe this cluster of symptoms is caused by wanting to avoid the intense pain; most of them are ways to separate from oneself. My symptoms were as follows: (1, 2, 3) I experienced avoidance at various times, especially for the first six months after the birth; (4) diminished interest in significant activities was true for a much longer period, as I withdrew my energies from my community and family; (5) estrangement was felt until I found others who would listen to my story without trying to tell me how lucky I was to have a healthy baby; (6) restricted affect was not so much of a problem for me, as I tend to have feelings on and above the surface (however, many new mothers report a numbness of all feelings); (7) the sense of a foreshortened future still haunts me after almost five years. Because I lived through this event I now know that unfortunate things do happen; babies do die. For many months after Evan's birth, I stated to my spouse and a few friends that if it weren't for his being alive, I would want to die; I did not believe that I would ever recover from his birth. In my experience, the sense of a foreshortened future is a reflection of the new mother's despair, the sense of a black hole that will swallow her.

The DSM-III-R describes other symptoms of PTSD.

> D. Persistent symptoms of increased arousal (not present before the trauma), as indicated by at least two of the following:

(1) difficulty falling or staying asleep
(2) irritability or outbursts of anger
(3) difficulty concentrating
(4) hypervigilance
(5) exaggerated startle response
(6) physiologic reactivity upon exposure to events that symbolize
    or resemble an aspect of the traumatic event (e.g., a woman
    who was raped in an elevator breaks out in a sweat when
    entering any elevator)

The following points correspond to the above:

1. I recall my fourth night at the hospital when I acquired mobility, no longer hooked up to an IV, walking a circle around the ward, all night long. I walked and walked, and wondered if I would ever sleep peacefully again. That type of night happened periodically.

2. Outbursts of anger happened, and again, these responses are a part of healing. This symptom is often expressed; though anger or irritability directed at loved ones in an inappropriate or mean way causes secondary problems.

3. I can most vividly recall difficulty concentrating at work, as I returned to my office when Evan was five weeks old. It took close to a year to regain my mental acuity.

4. I was hypervigilant about Evan, fearful of any threat to his well-being, and particularly fearful that he would stop breathing. I was also hypervigilant toward myself, afraid to be touched, afraid of what my body would go through next.

5. An exaggerated startle response was not one of my symptoms. It frequently occurs after an experience, and may manifest as fear of a surprise attack. For example, an incision was made without warning or one's body was mishandled or restrained, and as a consequence, the individual is "jumpy" afterwards.

6. I had distinct physiologic reactions when birth was being discussed; I would hyperventilate and become clammy. When Evan was more than a year old, I returned to the hospital where he was born for a different purpose. I could not visit the maternity ward in an attempt to desensitize myself; I had a complete panic reaction.

Other symptoms listed by the DSM-III-R include:

E. Duration of the disturbance (symptoms in B, C, and D) of at least one month.

Specific delayed onset if the onset of symptoms was at least six months after the trauma.

In my case, this trauma lasted well into a second year; not as intense as time went on, but I could still meet the above criteria. Women who suppress their responses could have a delayed onset, well beyond six months.

Put in understandable language, a person experiences shock and horror, with responses similar to someone who has undergone a natural disaster such as a tornado, severe physical abuse, or war. The diagnosis was developed from treating war veterans, and though not often applied to a new mother, it could be when the birth has been traumatic from an unexpected or difficult cesarean or other interventions, or when the baby has died. Trauma is trauma, and its identification is one more way of acknowledging the power and importance of the birth experience.

Trauma in this context in some cases must be acknowledged as an aspect of medicine gone awry; an unnecessary cesarean is an example of iatrogenic treatment, meaning treatment by the physician that has resulted in disease. PTSD could be diagnosed by the same doctors who caused or contributed to the disorder, during a visit for postpartum distress or depression. It is unlikely that this discussion would take place with an obstetrician. A third-party therapist or other practitioner is a more likely resource.

Uncovering strong emotions, acknowledging trauma, and integrating the events into a woman's life aid her healing. Some therapists and obstetricians refer women to a psychiatrist for medication to relieve or suppress anxiety or depression. This situation can be similar to the denial of pain and use of medication during labor. The personal choice of using or not using medication needs to be honored. Medication for emotional pain can give a woman a break from the intensity of her situation and free her to look at the situation more clearly. For some, medication prolongs denial and suppression of images and emotions that need to emerge.

It is natural to want to avoid unpleasant emotions and memories. If they are deeply buried, a woman is at risk for berating herself for having trouble uncovering them and acknowledging that they are part of her. Feelings and memories seem to have lives of their own; they emerge when a person is ready to experience them. The job is to meet them halfway. If the symptoms outlined above are experienced, with or without specific memories, this path of healing is a necessary one. There is no effective shortcut.

Keep in mind that PTSD does not define a person, only a state of being that changes and modifies depending on how a person copes. PTSD is a dangerous label if it is used to remain stuck in the trauma, as a way to stay victimized. In addition, two women can undergo similar experiences and have remarkably different outcomes. History is also a factor.

Any diagnosis has potential to be misused, and can be a label that enables a woman to act victimized or powerless. If therapy is pursued and something like this happens, talk with the therapist to discuss the purpose of the diagnosis, including whether it is a helpful tool. Discussing ways of avoiding any label will help empower the individual and encourage more beneficial therapy. If a woman decides the diagnosis fits her response and behavior and she is comfortable with it, then she can negotiate the kind of help she wants. If she doesn't get the response she's looking for or answers to her questions, another therapist can be sought. Or, where a diagnosis is not necessary, other therapeutic options exist with a spiritual director or other non-insurance-based professional who is paid out of pocket.

The PTSD diagnosis is most useful as a tool of recovery, one of many that guides a woman through difficult times. When doubts occur that what happened to her was traumatic, recalling the characteristics of PTSD is helpful. If a woman has nightmares about the birth, or terrifying thoughts come into her mind unbidden, this tool will help her know that she is not crazy, but she is recovering from trauma. These responses, though unpleasant, exist and are part of healing.

TWO OTHER BIRTH STORIES

Vicky and Ellen are two women whose babies were born under circumstances that many people would consider normal deliveries. Their stories depict births involving different interventions for different reasons. As a result, the quality of their healing varies. Yet they are on common ground in many ways. Neither had outlets for relating what happened to them. Their expectations were shattered. Unexpected physical procedures were done, with lasting impact. Their self-confidence was shaken. Vicky's and Ellen's stories are followed throughout the book, highlighting different responses and ways to heal. In this chapter, the actual births are related. As their stories unfold, note the characteristics of posttraumatic stress disorder. Vicky's story is told first.

I went to Dr. Harvey, the obstetrician referred by my mother. He delivered me, and I never even thought of going to anybody else. I had never even seen a doctor before for an annual checkup. So we went there, and thinking back, he didn't answer a lot of my questions. When I'd say, "I read in the books some doctors give enemas, do you give enemas?" He'd say, "Oh, don't you worry your pretty little head about anything," "I'll take care of you, I'll take care of you." Well, I thought, I'll go in and have my baby, and I don't have to like or dislike you, it's just about me and Greg and the baby.

I'm afraid of doctors, I always have been, and at the prenatals the nurse would always take my blood and then take my blood pressure. My blood pressure was always high, and I'd say, "That's because you just pricked my finger and I saw blood." You know, don't do that. The nurse took the blood pressure again during the exam a couple of times at the beginning of the pregnancy, and it always went down considerably when it was taken at the end of the exam.

I started to get some swelling at the end of my pregnancy, around thirty-six weeks. I went in and my blood pressure was slightly elevated but nothing to be concerned about. Dr. Harvey said, "Why don't you go home and lay around and just take it easy?" I did, and I went in for a non-stress test and it turned out fine. My blood pressure went back to normal, so I'm thinking the one time my blood pressure was high, was after they had just pricked my finger, and then they didn't take it again. I didn't think to tell them to retake it.

The next time I went in, because of the blood pressure Dr. Harvey said, "Why don't you have your baby on Thursday?" I was only at thirty-seven weeks. I said, "How would I do that?" He said, "You come in and I'll induce you. You'll get pitocin through an IV, I'll give you an epidural, and then you'll have your baby." He told me to come in to Cedar Hospital on Thursday. I said we didn't choose Cedar as our hospital. We had chosen another one we liked better. He said, "I really like Cedar, and I'll be there on Thursday, so you just come in."

I went home and said, "Greg, no way, I'm not going to do this." He said, "Why not? Wouldn't it be nice to know when you're going to have your baby?" I said, "Well, I'm not going to have an epidural." So I called the doctor up and said to cancel the order on that, I'm not going to have that. But I did agree to come in as scheduled.

I went to the hospital three weeks early, and there was no real reason for it. My blood pressure was not elevated, and if you look at my medical records, during the entire labor my blood pressure was not elevated. An elevated blood pressure was the only reason the birth was scheduled early.

On Thursday morning I was looking forward to it, I wasn't

scared or worried at all because I knew it would go smoothly. We got to the hospital and I put on the little gown, and the nurse came in and started the pitocin. The doctor came in and broke my water at about nine o'clock, and that was the last time I saw him until five o'clock. My labor started about an hour later I guess, it was pretty heavy. An epidural was scheduled for when I reached five centimeters, whether I wanted it or not. And I said, "No, I don't want it."

I had been getting up every hour or every half hour just to get up. I used needing to go to the bathroom as my excuse. I had the monitors on and everything, and I think they got tired of hooking me back up, so I was told, "I'm sorry, you can't get up any more." Then I got a really bad headache from laying there, and was told, "We'll give you something for your headache." I took the drugs because my headache was worse than the labor pains, it was blurring my vision. I think I got the headache because I couldn't get up and move around. The drugs didn't do anything for the labor pains, of course. At five centimeters they came in with everything for the epidural, and I said I didn't want it. There was an argument about that. First the nurse said, "We'll come back in half an hour." Then the nurse said, "It's on your chart, you need to have it." So being the good little patient I was, not realizing I could say no, I went through with the epidural. I don't think it actually stopped or affected my labor because it kept progressing.

At eight and a half centimeters I was really relaxed, I was just laying there handling it. Greg went down to supper and I was just there relaxing. The nurse came in and when she checked me said, "Oh, my gosh, this baby's head's coming right down, everything's moving along, this baby's going to be born soon." She set up the trays in my room, and then said, "I've been a nurse for so many years, and usually it takes a couple hours to push the baby out, so probably about eight o'clock you'll have your baby."

As she was getting the trays ready and saying all this stuff about how good it's going, Dr. Harvey walked in. He didn't talk to her or check me or anything. He said, "I'm sorry, Vicky, this isn't working, we have to do a c-section right away." I said, "What's the matter?" He said, "Well, the baby's head isn't coming down." And the nurse slammed down her tray and looked at him, and I knew he never checked me, how would he know the baby's head wasn't coming down? I hadn't seen him since nine o'clock that morning, and I knew that wasn't the nurse's opinion, she had just said the opposite to me. So I said, "No, I'm not having a c-section." He said, "You have a half hour to progress to ten." The nurse walked out of the room mad, slamming the door, and I said, "I'm not having this done, just get out of here." And then he walked out and I heard him arguing with the nurse.

When the nurse came back in she started taking my barrettes out, my jewelry off, grabbing at me, and I said, "Get away from me, go get my husband right now." She said, "Oh, there's enough time, don't worry about it." Her attitude had totally changed out in the hallway. I think Dr. Harvey put her in her place because she wasn't in agreement with what he was doing. I said, "Well, this isn't going to happen." She said, "You'll be all right, these things happen." And her attitude had totally changed from yes, this baby's head has come down.

Then Greg walked into the room. Dr. Harvey had intercepted him in the hallway and had said, "We've got to get this baby out right now, its head is too big, it's just a really bad situation." So Greg came in all hyper, and I said, "Greg, that's not the case, the baby is fine, I was hooked up to all the monitors, that's not why. Dr. Harvey just wants to go home." It took a few minutes to convince Greg, tell him the story, and I said, "You have to get someone to help me." He went running around the hospital as they were shaving my crotch. I couldn't do anything to stop them, every two minutes I was having contractions. I was doing as much as I could, but every two minutes I had to stop. As I was yelling they tied me down to the cart and started rolling me down the hall. My half hour wasn't even up, so I was yelling and screaming at the top of my lungs for them to stop while Greg was running around, trying to find someone to help him. He said it was as though everybody just hid under their desks, it was a totally empty hospital, and he didn't know where to go. I was yelling, "Get the foot doctor, get the eye doctor, I don't care, just get someone to help me." My mom had come up during that half hour, and I said, "Mom, you've got to help me." My mom is a nurse, and she said, "I would never go against a doctor." That was the last person I saw, and Greg came into the operating room as they were starting to get me ready, saying, "I'm sorry, I'm sorry, I'm dressed for the surgery, and I didn't know what to do to stop it."

I was still having contractions, and I could feel them. I could feel pushing, I had to push, so I don't know if the meds ever were working. I was hysterical, I was shaking, screaming, and I kept hearing the anesthesiologist saying, "Is this girl in pain, or is she just upset?" And no one answered him, I didn't answer him. He kept saying, "What's wrong with her?" They put the urinary catheter in and I said, "Stop, I felt that. Guys, this isn't working. Is this my anesthesia, is this what I'm going on?" The anesthesiologist said yes. I said I felt the catheter totally. So he said, "Someone get me an ice cube." He put it on my stomach and started rubbing it. I said, right, left, up, down. I said, "Wait a second, I can feel this." The doctor said, "What's going on here?" The anesthesiologist said something's not working, and the doctor said, "I don't have time for this," and he started cutting.

My hands were tied down, and I felt everything. I was still yelling. The doctor said, "Isn't there a way to shut her up?" He said he wanted to use—I don't know the medical names, and the anesthesiologist said, "You shouldn't give that with an epidural." Dr. Harvey said, "I don't care, it's my responsibility," or something like that. So they put a mask over my face, it was bubble gum gas like from the dentist's office, and that's the only anesthesia I had through the surgery, and it obviously didn't do anything more than shut me up, because the mask was over my mouth.

The surgery nurse had just bought a house in Golden Valley, and her carpet was green wall-to-wall carpet, it has four bedrooms upstairs, two baths, this was her whole conversation, I know the whole layout of the house perfectly. They talked the whole time to each other. No one ever spoke to me, no one said, we're doing this, your baby's almost out, here we go. No one talked to Greg, even. No one. Except he had a nurse standing by him to take care of him. I had no one standing by me to take care of me. No one spoke to me, it was as if I wasn't even there. And then Jack was born, as I was still screaming through my mask. They never even said, "Your baby's here." They brought him over to the warming table, and his first Apgars were nine and ten, he wasn't in distress. He didn't need to be born this way. They didn't hold him up for me to see him. I kept saying, "What is it? what is it?" No one answered. Greg had to get up and go over to the warming table and yell back to me, "It's our baby, Vicky, it's our baby." I didn't know if it was a boy or a girl. Greg was a father just out of his head looking at the baby. Finally he brought him over and said he's a boy, and I saw him for one second. There's no reason except for hospital protocol for that, and then they continued talking about this house. No one ever said, blood pressure this, or Apgar that, not even that. It was like they were sitting around playing cards. No one said, are you okay, the baby's here, it's gorgeous, we're going to sew you up now, you're all done—it was as if I wasn't there. Then I said I wanted to see the placenta, and they all started laughing, I don't know why, whether it was what they were talking about or if it was what I said. And then I looked up at the anesthesiologist and said, "Can you put me to sleep now?" At first he said, no, but I begged him, I didn't even care if I wasn't going to see Jack for awhile. I said, "Please, just put me to sleep." He said, "I can't." After a while, he did.

The Thursday of my c-section was Labor Day weekend, and Dr. Harvey had Friday, Saturday, Sunday, and Monday off. He was on call Thursday night, and I was the only person in labor at the two hospitals he covers. The medical secretary was very helpful in finding out all this information.

After I was in my hospital room, no one would answer the intercom, even though I kept asking for my baby. Finally a nurse came and brought him. While I held him, she read me the whole hospital policy manual, about how to use the bedpan and use the squeeze bottle to wash my perinium. Well, my perinium didn't need to be washed off because it was never used. She gave me the little bag of sanitary pads, compliments of the hospital, and left me with Jack. Then they kept taking Jack back to the nursery, and I said, no, he stays with me, and they said, we want you to rest. I didn't have any strength to fight. As it turned out I never felt good, and ended up with a severe infection. I woke up in the middle of the night after Jack was born, just shaking, I was so sick with a terrible pain that was as bad as the surgery pain. It was an infection. I had lost so much blood my hemoglobin count was down to seven, and it had started at twelve.

I had five IVs going into my body, they were all different antibiotics, because it was a very horrible infection. The infection raged, and my veins weren't very good. At the end there was only one IV. They wanted to send me home on IVs, and I refused. I couldn't take care of Jack properly, I couldn't change his diaper or anything. They'd come in with a towel and say, get up and take your shower, and I couldn't even stand up, my stomach hurt so bad because it was still so full of infection. I think it was a staph infection. Greg had to lift me out of bed. I walked for a month totally hunched over because my stomach was so infected, I couldn't stand up.

The only good thing that came out of it was that I was so sick I didn't do anything but hold Jack and nurse him, that's the only good thing that came out of it. I think we made up for the bonding that didn't occur during birth because I couldn't do anything else but hold him after he was born. I had five different antibiotics, Greg had to go buy pill containers because I couldn't keep track, and I'm a pretty organized person. I was assured the antibiotics wouldn't hurt Jack, but I don't know how all the drugs could not have affected him since I was nursing. I was really physically sick, mentally sick, too. Afterwards, the nurses were very good, as supportive as they could be. I don't think they understood the emotional things but they knew how sick I was. They were kind, very kind, they had never had anyone that sick before. Infections from cesareans are not uncommon, but I had an extreme infection.

The medical secretary came in, she happens to be an acquaintance. She came into my room at the end of her shift, and said, "I heard what happened, Vicky, these guys are a bunch of clowns. When a woman walks in on a Friday or a holiday in labor, we all look at each other, 'Oh oh, there's another c-section, we'd better gown up right now.'" She said they were the worst o.b. group, and were reprimanded five years ago. They improved somewhat, but now they're backsliding because they're not being monitored any more.

The day after my c-section another nurse came in. She put her hand over her name tag and said, "This happens all the time." Those two people couldn't support me officially, but they let me know I was not alone, because I was screaming my head off the whole time, what the hell happened to me, why did they let him do this, get this pig out of my room. He came into my room to take out the staples, and he said, "Oh, I did a beautiful job, you'll be wearing a bikini pretty soon." Well, I'm not the bikini type, and I told him I don't wear bikinis. When I asked why this happened, Dr. Harvey said, "Well, honey, that baby just wouldn't fit."

The main thing was that Jack's head was so engaged, his head was really molded. My mom is a nurse and when she saw him she thought something was wrong with him. But it was from being in the birth canal because he was trying to come out. He was on his way out, and his head had to be pulled back out through the uterus. I don't think it affected him, he is very smart. It could have affected him emotionally in many ways.

Then everybody said to me, "Oh, who cares how your baby was born, he's here, he's here. Who cares?" No one understood. Greg's answer was, "You just have to forget about it. You just have to forget. I know it was awful, I was there, but you just have to for- get about it, because it's not going to do any good to sit around and mope about it." The only thing I wanted to do was sit in a closet with Jack. I had to say to myself, only psycho people sit in closets, you're not going to sit in the closet, because then you'd be psycho. You can sit here by the closet and look in there and say, yeah, that's where I want to be. I'd look into my linen closet and want to be in there because then I'd be okay. There were no groups that I could go to, there was nothing. I thought I was the only person in the world who had suffered an unnecessary c-section. I did not have a clue that it was an epidemic. Every night I cried myself to sleep, I cried in my sleep. I'd wake up shaking and screaming.

Though there was no evidence according to Vicky that her baby was in danger, she and the baby were treated as though this were true, creating a traumatic scenario. Additionally, the physical treatment of Vicky induced severe trauma. The transition from labor to an operation when Vicky was ignored and discounted shattered Vicky's world as she knew it, creating severe emotional trauma. Vicky knew there was something wrong immediately, although she received little validation from others. Her sense of violation, intrusion, and despair were instantly on the surface. She was haunted from that first day with strong symptoms of trauma, and her healing journey was volatile.

Ellen's story is quite different; her trauma is not as dramatic, yet her vision of what was going to happen was entirely different from what actually did. Ellen's reactions to the birth were more low-key, yet she required as much attention afterwards in order to feel competent and whole again.

I woke up about three o'clock in the morning with mild labor, and I got up and came out and sat in a cozy chair and read my books. I was too excited to go back to sleep. But I finally did after sitting up for about two hours and slept fitfully, not because of the pain but because I was too excited, too worked up. I got up that morning and told my grandma and Matt that I was in labor, and we just did things around the house that morning. I took a bath, washed my hair and put it up in a braid so I wouldn't have to deal with it at the hospital. I got some last minute things together. Then we ate lunch, my grandma made chicken soup, she thought that would be a nice thing to eat.

I wanted to put off going to the hospital until the last possible moment, and felt like I had. The doctor had told me to come in when the contractions were five minutes apart and I waited till they were three. It was about two o'clock when we went to the hospital and we still got there early. I hadn't been at the hospital very long, and I lost my lunch. That was the first thing that happened to me. I hadn't had any nausea at all during the pregnancy, I hadn't thrown up at all, so throwing up made me feel like a patient. I thought my body was betraying me, I couldn't even keep my lunch down. I know now my experience wasn't all that uncommon. It's hard to think of it as a natural event that my body just couldn't handle food right then, rather than my body betraying me. It upset me. Then I had that taste in my mouth. I thought the hospital wasn't going to let me eat, and now I would get real hungry. I don't like being hungry. But you're so busy with what you're doing that you don't notice hunger, and they did let me drink.

I think they monitored me for awhile when I first got there, but then they let me get up and wander around the ward. As I walked I had to lean against the railing because of the back labor. We hadn't been there long when I asked if I could go in the whirlpool. It must be something not asked for very often, but they cooperated, and it was good. It felt a lot better to be in the whirlpool. But I felt like I needed to be doing something, I wanted to manage the labor. It wasn't enough to just sit there and let the labor happen, so I didn't stay in the whirlpool very long. Looking back I think it was a very productive time.

At about ten o'clock they checked me. When I went in I was at two centimeters, and at ten o'clock I was only at four. I thought I should have made a lot more progress. I was getting tired, and at that point I was worried about getting sleep. I was worried that I would be too tired to push the baby out. So the nurses convinced me that I should have an amniotomy, that it would increase the contractions, get the labor moving. Matt and I talked about it, I didn't really want to do it because I knew that was the beginning of the slippery slope of interventions. I just really didn't want to, but on the other hand I was really tired, so I agreed. A doctor I had never seen before or since came in with the long crochet hook and broke the bag of waters.

It did increase contractions, and they got so strong that I couldn't handle them anymore. At that point they started talking about pain medication. I had read and talked to different people, and had it in my mind that if I did have pain medication I would start with demerol, just something to take the edge off the pain, that wouldn't completely put me out of commission. Well, they convinced me that if I had an epidural I would be able to sleep. And that was the magic word for me, sleep. I agreed to it and went ahead and had the epidural done. I had a catheter inserted in the lower region of my back, an IV for electrolytes or something for my metabolism I guess, and a blood pressure cuff on the other arm. I also had on an external monitor, and I think at that point they put on the internal monitor, and a bladder catheter. I had wires everywhere. By then I felt totally like a patient. I wasn't able to get out of bed any more. I remember I could feel the contractions a little bit at the top of my uterus, but that was it.

I hung out the rest of the night. At one point they called in the obstetrician because they were worried about the baby's heartbeat. The o.b. looked at the monitor strip and she decided that something had to be done. At that point she said she was concerned I might

need to have a cesarean. That and an episiotomy were the two
things I'd hoped to avoid. She said that we could try oxygen, that
might help the baby. So I put on an oxygen mask, which didn't
seem invasive at all. It worked, the oxygen straightened his heart
rate out. Then I slept pretty well, on and off. I was amazed when
they checked me about seven thirty, and I was fully dilated. How
could that be? I hadn't felt anything. They started wheeling in the
baby warmer and all their junk, and that's when I started getting
excited again, because I realized this was really it. I guess I thought
the baby would be there in a half an hour. Little did I know.

I told them to turn off the epidural, because I wanted to be
able to feel to push. I didn't know how long that would take, but I
think it takes about an hour. They went ahead and told me to start
pushing, and I felt absolutely no urge, but I thought I'd better cooperate. They'd tell me when I was having a contraction, and I could
feel it tightening a little at the top, so there was a little sensation.
Something seemed goofy to me about when they would tell me to
push, but I just kept cooperating. I wanted to be upright and tried to
push that way for quite awhile, but nothing much was happening.
Then they made me recline, and I knew that was bad but I cooperated. They did break away the bottom of the bed, so theoretically I
could squat. But I wasn't. My feet were touching the part of the bed
that was lowered, but it didn't feel like I was doing anything. Then
the obstetrician told me to frog my legs, get them up, basically in
the squat position but while lying on my back, so I didn't have gravity to help. At that point the nurse had one leg and Matt had the
other leg, and I think I had my feet on their chests, while they held
my legs. I was hanging onto the rails of the bed with my hands, and
I hung on so hard I got callouses on them and where my rings are
got pinched. I just pushed as hard as I could, and I thought, I'm
going to get hemorrhoids really bad, I just know it. I could tell that I
was pushing harder than I should have been pushing, because I
didn't feel any urge to be doing it.

That went on for a couple of hours, and it was finally at the
two-hour mark of pushing that the doctor decided to use the vacuum extractor. I was glad about that instead of using forceps,
because I'd heard horrible things about forceps. I was born with
them, with bruises and stuff. She was trying to put the vacuum
extractor on, and she turned it on, and it popped off, and blood was
flying everywhere. It whipped around and hit Matt in the leg, so he
was covered in blood, too. I don't know whether she had done the
episiotomy by then in order to use the vacuum extractor, but I didn't
feel it at all.

I'm not real clear why, but she thought it was necessary to have the nurses apply fundal pressure. They were pressing really hard at the top of my uterus to push the baby out. It was like squishing the bottom of a tube of toothpaste. I think about how small I am, and the baby was almost ten pounds. She finally did get the extractor on and pulled him out.

I had asked them to set up a mirror at the bottom of the bed so I could watch him being born, and when I looked down there was blood everywhere. Then he was finally out, and I got to look at him about half a second before they took him over to the baby warmer and started working on him, to suction out the mucous. They said the mucous was cloudy and he needed to be transported to the transitional nursery. I was bummed. When four hours went by and I still didn't have my baby, I was really bummed. But I figured they knew what was best. Matt went along and he said the baby was okay, but he needed to be watched because of the cloudy mucous. What is cloudy mucous?

They wanted me to get up, and I could not get up. I tried to and fainted, they let me get back down in bed. They wanted to move me out of the birthing room and get me into the recovery area, or whatever you call it. I couldn't do it. So they brought me my lunch, eating felt really good, because I was really hungry. I made a few phone calls telling people he was born. Then they finally got me out of the birthing room with a wheel chair. They still wanted me to walk, but I couldn't. I think it was because I lost so much blood. I was anemic when they finally tested my blood. My hemoglobin was at eight, and it had been fourteen, so my head would swim every time I stood up. I still would have to have help walking when I went to the bathroom later.

They moved me to a double room, and I had asked for a private one. The lady in there had had a cesarean after being on bedrest for six months, she had had a car wreck and her pelvis was broken. That put the whole thing in perspective for me, I didn't feel so bad for myself. She was really nice, she just had her third daughter, and she had been hoping for a boy. Someone had brought her little boy socks, so she gave them to me. Matt had gone home after Jason was born, he had been up all night. It was about four o'clock P.M. when I finally got to see Jason. They brought him in to me, and he nursed right away, he was a little barracuda thing, and that went really well. They moved me to a private room later that night, and my mom and grandma and other relatives came to visit. I was starting to feel better.

My mom and grandma were here for the first week, and I

remember telling them all about it. I guess I didn't feel they were as sympathetic as they should have been. I felt like I had been through a real traumatic thing, it hadn't worked out the way I wanted it to, and it wasn't a natural childbirth at all. All they said was the standard line, "You have a healthy baby," which felt really wrong, because it wasn't how I felt. They were just telling me I should feel all right.

A few days after the birth, mom and grandma went shopping, and Matt and I were alone with Jason for the first time. I burst into tears, sobbing. In retrospect, it was a little episode of postpartum depression, and I just lost it, I was a mess, I sat there sobbing and sobbing, and Matt asked me what was wrong. I felt overwhelmed by my new responsibilities, and everything that had happened to me, I felt like a victim. I felt like I had been taken advantage of. Especially when I had tried to insure everything would go as I wanted. I had a female obstetrician, and had let her know my intentions. I had written up a birth plan. I told her the things that I wanted and things that I didn't want. I'd done all kinds of reading. Sheila Kitzinger's, *Your Baby Your Way*, it's a good book, it showed me how to draw up a birth plan. I had read that thoroughly during my pregnancy, and reread it before the birth, so I thought I knew what I needed to know. And I just didn't. I was really disappointed that I hadn't been able to work the actual birth out the way I wanted. People didn't understand that. Nobody understood it at all until I went to ICAN (International Cesarean Awareness Network). Nobody was sympathetic. If you told them you had a bad time, they would tell you either some worse thing that happened to them, or they would minimize it and say, well, you have a healthy baby. It was really hard, I didn't feel like I had a lot of support. I started to believe I was wrong, I was making more out of it, and I was trying to make myself think the way that they were thinking—like, well, maybe I should feel better, it could have been a lot worse. I'd tell myself at least I didn't have a cesarean. I guess it worked for awhile to get it out of my mind, but I never felt like I could get any resolution, and I don't know if there is a resolution.

In some ways, Ellen's healing tasks were more difficult, as she birthed vaginally, and technically her birth would be considered natural. This disparity between how she felt and how the birth was presented to her is a crazy-making dynamic. Only when Ellen began talking with other women and exercising stronger influence on her choices of caregiver, hospital, and so forth, did she feel understood and whole again. The concept of trauma was not provided at the time of birth; eventually she had to seek it out.

Throughout the rest of the book, trauma is assumed to have occurred to Vicky and Ellen, and to other women whose stories are included. This chapter is a reference point whenever doubts arise as to whether what occurred requires attention and intervention. Physical or emotional traumatic birth events deserve care and understanding regardless of any external measure of their degree of damage. Ellen later told me that the hours of separation from her newborn baby may have been the worst part of the birth. Few sources of acknowledgment exist for that type of trauma or loss. If an individual identifies with these stories yet her birth was close to a dream birth, expand the definition of trauma to encompass her own experience.

FOR WORK ON YOUR OWN

Question One: Do I doubt that what happened to me was traumatic?

Question Two: What messages do I receive from others, either now or voices from the past that can still be heard in my head, that encourage me to minimize or completely discount the trauma?

Question Three: How am I afraid of my own responses to the trauma? For example, am I afraid of my dreams, images, daydreams, feelings? What am I afraid will happen if these responses are allowed full expression?

Question Four: Have I ever related all remembered details of my baby's birth to another person? If I have, how did it feel? If I haven't, am I comfortable with my story remaining inside myself and not sharing it with others?

FOR FURTHER READING

Medical Training and Information

Harrison, Michelle. (1982) *A Woman in Residence*. New York: Random House.
Jack, Dana Crowley. (1991) *Silencing the Self: Women and Depression*. Cambridge, MA: Harvard University Press.
Pekkanen, John. (1988) *M.D. Doctors Talk about Themselves*. New York: Delacorte.

Posttraumatic Stress Disorder

American Psychiatric Association. (1987) *DSM-III-R: Diagnostic and Statistical Manual, Third Edition, Revised.* Washington, D.C.: American Psychiatric Association.
Herman, Judith. (1992) *Trauma and Recovery: The Aftermath of Violence—from Domestic Abuse to Political Terror.* New York: Basic Books.

Cesarean Information

Cohen, Nancy. (1991) *Open Season: A Survival Guide for Natural Childbirth and VBAC in the 90s.* Westport, CT: Bergin & Garvey.
Cohen, Nancy Wainer, and Estner, Lois. (1983) *Silent Knife: Cesarean Prevention and Vaginal Birth after Cesarean (VBAC).* Westport, CT: Bergin & Garvey.
Marieskind, Helen. (1972) *An Evaluation of Cesarean Section in the United States: A Report to the Department of Health, Education and Welfare.* Washington, D.C.: Department of Health, Education and Welfare.
VanTuinen, Ingrid, and Wolfe, Sidney. (1992) *Unnecessary Cesarean Sections: Halting a National Epidemic.* Washington, D.C.: Public Citizen's Research Group.

ANOTHER KIND OF TRAUMA: DISTANCE FROM PEOPLE WHEN THEIR SUPPORT IS MOST NEEDED

The baby is ten weeks old, the scar is no longer raw and tender, though still red and sore at times. Or the episiotomy is healed, according to the doctor. You've been back at work for three weeks, day care has worked out all right, and you only have fifteen pounds to lose. So what do you have to complain about?

A woman faces everyone else's denial when she attempts to say how a traumatic birth has affected her. An uncomfortable sense of isolation and a fear of being crazy results, as loved ones, friends, and co-workers do not acknowledge her pain or how her world has changed. This separation from others in viewpoint and experience is often more difficult to heal than the physical wounds of birth. This postpartum dilemma happens regardless of the type of birth. A woman is expected to cope well with a new baby, and she is often overwhelmed instead.

"Most women have already resolved any issues they have about their births by the time they come see me for their postpartum checkup." An anonymous obstetrician seriously said these words to me during an inquiry about the need for emotional healing from traumatic births. I responded, "Maybe your patients' relationships with you are so important, they don't want to jeopardize them by telling you they're hurting about their births." Doctors still have so much power given to them that it is difficult to cross the threshold and speak out about the intimate event of birth, including any dissatisfaction, pain, or regrets. My observation is that at this time a woman could still be in shock, numb from what has happened, dumb with grief and rage.

This same dynamic occurs in other important relationships. The mother holds inside her real feelings and reactions, while those around her expect that life can now go on. "Leave the past behind you, it's time to move on." Aspects of life do go on, of course: baby grows, mother

physically heals, day-to-day details are tended. But the need for understanding has just begun, and a woman's search for it is like walking
through a minefield rather than a valid part of the grieving and healing process. Vicky stated:

> Maybe life goes on, but here I am, still bleeding inside. I don't
> know who to turn to, because everywhere I go, people turn away
> when I just hint at the birth being the horror that it was. One woman
> I know said, "I had two cesareans, both emergencies." Oh? I said,
> what were the emergencies? I thought, here was someone I could
> talk to. She said, "Dystocia. The babies were too big." I thought, oh
> no, she bought into it—I mean, it might have been true, but her
> babies were only around eight pounds.
>
> I couldn't talk to her about my misery and disappointment,
> she said what my mother says, "What matters is you have a healthy
> baby. What's the big deal going through surgery? People have
> surgery all the time." This woman thought it was easier to recover
> from surgery than to go through with labor. As though she avoided
> something really unpleasant, she got away with something.

Sometimes bonding is thwarted by birth trauma and frequent or
prolonged separations after birth between mother and baby. When
statements regarding how lucky a woman is to have a healthy baby are
made, her true feelings of anger and her desire to push the baby away
are further pushed inward. It took Judy, from chapter 1, several
months before she approached her baby with anticipation instead of
dread.

> Am I crazy? I hated my baby. I wanted no part in her baby-
> hood. I didn't want to hold her for the first two months of her life.
> Roger would put Julia in my arms, and I wouldn't look at her. The
> cesarean birth movie we saw in the birth class showed a couple
> smiling and happy with their baby. I wanted to leave mine in the
> hospital. As though she was one big mistake, a growth I could cut
> from me, sever the connection like the cesarean severed me. It
> would have been better if she had died. . . . I say all these things
> knowing I love her now, but God help me, I felt it then. I would let
> her cry, not for hours, but for good long times, I'd shut the door, and
> sit there in front of the TV, wishing I didn't have to take care of this
> baby.

Judy could not find a place to express her concerns about not
bonding with her baby. At her six-week checkup, her obstetrician told
Judy that she had postpartum depression, to give herself time, that
these feelings would pass. He offered Judy antidepressants. Her doc-

tor made no connection between the cesarean birth and lack of bonding, though many women experientially acknowledge this connection. Not until several months after Judy and Roger came in for couples counseling did she admit to anger toward her baby, and even deeper feelings. Then, the paradox of acknowledging feelings worked its magic; once Judy verbally blurted out her hatred, she felt closer to her daughter, not further apart. She began to see how the grief and betrayal experienced over Julia's birth needed to be expressed. She realized it was within herself, and not about her baby. Judy also had grief over how much time passed before she acknowledged the estrangement from her daughter. She wished she could turn the clock back to the birth, but that opportunity was gone.

Betrayal by her doctor, labor support, family, her body—any or all of these contribute to a woman's sense of failure. She failed at giving birth to her baby, so how can she be a good mother? Her body didn't do what it was supposed to, so she might as well gain fifty pounds and stop exercising, because what's the use? Her doctor told her everything would be fine, and according to the doctor, everything is fine—so she must be wrong. But damned if she will ever set foot in that doctor's office again. The article she read about labor coaches and husbands' involvement said there was a much higher rate of natural births if they were present—why was she the exception? Thoughts such as these have a negative ripple effect.

Each time a woman is confronted with someone else's minimization, placation, or denial, she is tempted to take this craziness into herself rather than acknowledge that the situation is crazy. She becomes stronger as she learns to trust herself and name what is going on inside, to separate out which thoughts are her responsibility and which are others', and to rebuild bridges with people she cares about.

After my first birth, though the cesarean was necessary, I was apologetic and took on all responsibility for the event. My own mine field was also crowded with issues of combining work with motherhood. It took a long time to sort out which pangs of remorse and shame belonged to which issue:

My friend Ceci from California called three weeks after Evan's birth. The last time we talked was when I was in the early stages of labor. After ordering diaper service for us, she had told me how raspberry leaf tea ice chips had helped her labor, and how to make them. We did, and then forgot them when we left for the hospital. Since the birth I had not called many people, and she waited three weeks to call back. I was on the bed in the late afternoon, Evan was asleep in the bassinet. Ceci was calling when her own baby, Esther,

was down for a nap and Rowyn, her three year old was at nursery school. Ceci said, "I was afraid something had gone wrong."
"Something did. The baby's fine, but Ceci, we had an emergency cesarean. I still feel torn up about it—"
"What is important is you have a healthy baby. Put the experience behind you now, it could have been worse. You have the rest of your lives together. Isn't motherhood wonderful. . ."
I made a face at her into the phone. She may have been right, but her brusqueness wasn't what I wanted to hear. Yes, he could have died, I could have died. He could have been disabled, making things worse. But I had to keep my mouth open. If all she heard was pity, too bad.
I didn't even talk to Ceci about work. We talked about mothering, of course. She had stayed home since Rowyn was born. Probably the idea of returning to work seemed ludicrous to her. I felt so split, talking out of both sides of my mouth. I wanted to just be the mother, and was envious of her lifestyle.
If not for the cesarean, I would have been able to return to work at four weeks as planned. Ironically, it forced me to take more time off, and to realize how ridiculous my prebirth plan was. Catherine had said during a visit in the hospital, "The cesarean delivery was the only thing that'd make you slow down, Lynn. It was a blessing, because nothing else would have stopped you from running yourself into the ground."
I heard her words. But I asked Catherine, "You mean you don't think I failed, that I shouldn't have given in, that there wasn't something I could have done to have given birth?"
"You did give birth. I don't believe that at all. I could hardly believe your strength. No, the baby was in danger long before they took him, you had a lot of courage, Lynn."
Even with that kind of support I was still not accepting the cesarean, still apologizing for what happened. Couldn't people tell from my face that I'd given birth in a mucked-up way? That my baby, now an incredible eight pounds of pure love, was marked by my inability to function as a woman needed to, in order to give birth? At any time I could close my eyes and recall the confusion and horror that happened right before he was born, and the pain afterwards.
My apology was due to all that I knew about unnecessary cesareans. Determined not to be one of them, it was hard to believe I wasn't. When telling someone of the birth, I assumed they thought I probably wimped out, or chose to have the cesarean. So I always felt like I was lying, that the cesarean could have been prevented.

Instead of being grateful for a healthy baby, grateful for surgery that saved a life, I was worried about whether it was necessary. Ceci was right, but I wasn't ready to let the birth go or forgive myself so easily.

It is important to realize that others have their own reactions to a birth; a woman's personal reaction is right for her regardless of others'. She can seek out evidence that she failed, or evidence that she was caught in a difficult situation and did her personal best. If I believe in myself, then I can sort others' messages. I recognize an attack or denial for what it is, as well as recognize support. Ceci's response was not what I wanted to hear, but she did not destroy me. The bridge between us was easy to rebuild because I trusted myself, we could be honest about our differences, and we both valued our past and future together. When there is a relationship conflict, if support exists as well, then it is worth pursuing resolution.

SUPPORT FROM SPOUSES

Spouses' birth experiences and expectations are intrinsically different from a birthing woman's. Of course. Yet often spouses are the ones women first turn to for support, and the kind of understanding sought may be unrealistic. Spouses give support, but it won't be totally what a woman needs. They are too close to the situation, and have their own reactions and investments. Usually spouses are men, who of course have never given birth; they may have empathy, but not experience. Recognizing that different people give different kinds of support, or no support, marks the mines in the field. When a mine blows up, when support is not forthcoming, it won't be entirely unexpected. Then a woman can better recognize sources of support and make her search less random.

Vicky sought support from Greg constantly, until she realized that he could not provide for all her needs and she would need resources outside of the marriage.

I was in a grocery store, and I saw an article in a parenting magazine, called "The Incision Decision". I stood and read it in the store and started sobbing, everybody was looking at me, and I couldn't stop. I had to leave my grocery cart in the middle of the store and go home, and all I bought was this magazine. I showed it to Greg and said, "Look, it's real, it's not just me." It was taking a very big toll on him and me. I didn't really blame him for the cesarean happening, he was in no more control than I was, but his mechanism was to forget it, and he didn't want to hear me. And all I wanted to do was talk about it twenty-four hours a day. All I wanted to do was cry and have him hold me twenty-four hours a day, and instead we would fight and argue and yell.

I packed up my bags one night and got Jack ready. I knew I wasn't going to my mom's house, because she wouldn't listen to me. The only person I knew that would listen was my friend a hundred and fifty miles and three hours away. I said to Greg, "We're leaving to go to Kathy's. Until you can be a supportive person, I'm out of here." He said, "This is not worth it, are you going to let that doctor ruin our relationship? You let him ruin your life, your birth experience, now are you going to let him ruin us?" I said, "No, but I need you, where are you?" The turning point finally happened when I was standing at the door with my bags packed, at two-o'clock in the morning. Jack was four months old. I didn't leave, Greg was right. I couldn't let that doctor take away my relationship, too.

Then finally one day we were talking and Greg said, "Can't you just schedule a time for us to talk about it?" At first I thought what an ass, schedule time to talk about my life falling apart? And then I started thinking, my gosh, maybe he really doesn't have the energy, who does, to listen to me whine twenty-four hours a day. So we started to schedule times, and he really started understanding. There were certain books and things that I would bring home, and then he started evolving. But it almost ended us. Then he had said the part about scheduling time, and it worked for us. And then I thought, how selfish of me to want everyone to be in mourning. That was a bend in the road.

Having witnessed the birth, spouses have their own trauma to heal. Because of this, their ability to listen to and support the birthing woman is conceivable, but not always possible. Spouses have a different view of the entire birth experience—their bodies were not involved. Some even spent the first hours after birth alone with the newborn, and have a special bonding as a consequence of surgery or other intervention. Spouses may need to hang onto their faith with the medical practitioners for their own various reasons.

All of the above may be true, but spouses can still support a woman's journey through healing, even without understanding as comprehensively as she would like. In some cases, as in Vicky and Greg's, the couple needs to agree to disagree. To agree that their experiences were different. Communication lines need to be open to the degree that both partners can report their responses and progress in healing to one another. Acceptance of different challenges, timetables, and needs fosters a companionable partnership, one that allows each of them to seek other forms of support outside of the relationship. Vicky began that search with a call to the hospital about a resource listed in her information booklet.

> One day I was paging through a hospital handbook and it said "Resources," Cesarean Prevention Movement [now called International Cesarean Awareness Network, or ICAN]. I called up the hospital and asked what it was and the receptionist said, "Well, I don't know."
>
> I said, "It's right here in your handbook, don't you have a number or something?"
>
> "I don't have any idea what you're talking about."
>
> I said, "Open your book to page thirty-seven, and look up at the top, the fourth one down," and she said, "Oh, yeah, I don't know anything about it."
>
> Meanwhile, I said to myself, prevention? Who else wants to prevent these things but me? She gave me a number, and I called, and this person was willing to listen to me. I told her, "I feel like I've been raped, I can't look in the mirror, I can't be touched, what is wrong?" This person said, "That's the most common feeling." I said, "You're kidding, you're kidding me." So I was sent information, I went to the meetings, and a grieving and healing group. I thought at first, these are the only people in the whole world who had these experiences, and it's taken me a long time to realize that it's not just a few people.

Vicky's perseverance and desire to feel less emotional pain paid off. She eventually found others to talk to who did not minimize what had happened, and she stopped randomly seeking support. It is sometimes difficult to accept that different people give different things. With the emotionally loaded subject of birth, differences in philosophy and practice make for volatile encounters. Without the agreement to disagree with respect, primary relationships such as marriage, parent-daughter, and friendships can be torn apart.

SUPPORT FROM MOTHERS

Some women cannot discuss their births with their mothers. The potential for passing on wisdom and love is thwarted by the estrangement mother, daughter, or both feel within themselves about birth. Many women in the last fifty years have had intervened births. Prior to the increased rate of cesareans and interventions in the 1970s, mothers of current birthing women were often given general anesthe-

sia and were not conscious during the births of their babies. My own
mother had me by high forceps delivery. For her second baby she was
given anesthesia and was unconscious, and with her third baby she
was lucky and birthed naturally, watching herself in a mirror. At that
time, in the early sixties, she was an exception in giving birth without
more intervention.

Ellen was disappointed about not being able to discuss her first
birthing experience with her mother.

> Two days after Jason's birth, we went home. Matt and I were
> alone with Jason for the first time, and I started bawling, I don't
> know if it was the hormones because my milk was starting to come
> in, but I think it was my disappointment about all the birth stuff. I
> cried for three hours, and didn't stop until my mother and grand-
> mother came in. My grandmother is eighty, I didn't want to upset
> her. Matt seemed shell-shocked, he couldn't handle hearing any-
> thing about the birth. So I never talked to anyone about it. I tried
> with my mother, I really wanted her support, but she said to focus
> on my beautiful big baby, that I was lucky to have him, and the birth
> didn't matter. That was the most painful, that she couldn't listen to
> me.
>
> Maybe it was because my mother had me when she was
> completely knocked out, and didn't see me for hours afterward. I
> never thought about how I may have repeated my own birth, but it
> could be true.
>
> I didn't think that the kinds of things that happened to me ever
> happened to anyone else until I went to an ICAN meeting and heard
> similar stories. Then I heard how birth experiences could also be
> positive ones. I suppose the worst time, because it was such a con-
> trast, was when Jason was close to a year old, and my best friend
> had her baby in Scotland. She had a home birth, and she called me
> when the baby was two hours old. The midwives had left after
> cleaning up, and she had her baby in her arms. I realized all the
> things I had missed in Jason's birth. Not that my friend painted her
> labor as any picnic, it was hard, but she did the birth on her own.

Vicky, too, was disappointed by the lack of communication with
her mother.

> My mom has always been a real good mom, but she's a med-
> ical professional, and at the time when the birth was happening, she
> was at the hospital. She had come in when I was hysterical, and I
> said, "Please mom, go try to find another doctor." This was when
> Greg was running around trying to find one. I said, "This is not right,

you have to stop this." And she said, "I would never go against a doctor's wishes," and she walked out. Afterwards she would never talk about it. She said, "Oh, you've got your baby, who cares?" She never acknowledged what happened.

I went to her work a couple of weeks later, she wanted me to show off the baby. She drove me over there, and someone said, "Oh, I heard you had a rough time." I said, "Yeah, it was terrible," and started telling them about it. Mom stood behind me and made the o.k. sign and made a face, and I saw it because there was a mirror on the wall.

You know, there was no one at all that acknowledged it was a terrible experience, no one. Instead, people would say, "Who cares? How could you care, how could you be so selfish to care, you have your baby." I talked to everybody, family, friends, acquaintances at church, and no one would acknowledge how horrible my experience was. I told anybody that would listen, anybody who walked by and said, "You have a beautiful baby." "Yes, but do you know how he was born," I would reply, and I'd try to tell them how it wasn't right. And then I'd hear, "Oh, well, you have your nice baby, and how could it matter to you?"

Both Vicky and Ellen value their mothers and needed connection. Stoic and silent behavior between mother and daughter can result when the universal event of giving birth is swept under the carpet.

After my first birth, I did not discuss my disappointment about my birthing experience with my mother; she was supportive in other ways. She was there in the ways she could be at that time, providing help with the house and care for the baby. I had hoped for more closeness with her, but had become aware of our differences while on a visit during my pregnancy. These differences clearly appeared one day while doing errands.

As we were on our way to the store we drove by Julie Erikson's house. Mother said, "You know, Julie moved back in with her parents, she was having marriage difficulties."

I was surprised to hear this gossip, as I had thought of Julie as one of us who got her dream. "Wow, she has three kids, I wonder if they're all living there. Anne told me that at the ten-year high school reunion she won the prize for the most children." I used to see Julie and her boyfriend at the park, lying on the grass together with their van parked nearby. They married young. So few people at my high school had children in their twenties—Julie had three. *Three*. Here I was, just starting on my first baby fifteen years later.

"By the way, Sarah Peckinworth is pregnant again, she had

her first child with that British lawyer. They never got married. But now she seems to be settling down. This baby has a different father—a nice, stable college professor. I hope it works out for her. She could use some stability, her mother is very concerned."

I was glad that this time *I* was pregnant and when Mother got together with the bridge group she's played with since moving to that neighborhood thirty years ago, she'll have me to talk about. Maybe I'd even go to a high school reunion one of these years, now that I had something in common with the people I grew up with. Being pregnant, I believed I was entering the mainstream. In the sixth grade I fit in finally by getting a bra like the rest of the girls in class, though I didn't need one. In junior high getting a boyfriend was what made me feel like I'd arrived. Funny these were my measures, because being located near Stanford University and Silicon Valley, my high school fostered very educated students. I was an anomaly, as my parents were high school educated, and my father ran the garbage company for the city. I overcame some obstacles to get my Ph.D., and in an academic way would certainly belong with my old high school peers. But being pregnant was what made me feel that I belonged.

As we drove by the Elk's Club pool where I spent many childhood hours swimming in the summers, I asked my mother questions about her own and my aunt's pregnancies in the hopes I could foresee my own future. We drove down El Camino Real, past the bowling alley where she used to play in a league and I used to hang out in junior high. I asked if she had saved any baby things from us four children. I had this warm fantasy about her passing down quilts, clothes, bedding, and toys. She interrupted quickly and said, "I'm not sure, I think I've given most of those things away. Besides, I'm not ready to think about becoming a grandmother. This is going to take me awhile. Who do you think you are, anyway? Why did you tell us so soon, what if something goes wrong?" She looked ahead, her face tight, both hands on the steering wheel.

"I'm not just a little bit pregnant, Mom. And besides, I'd have wanted to tell you anyway, even if something had gone wrong." Ouch.

I sat there afraid of her. She rummaged in her purse for some gum, one hand on the steering wheel. I helped her, but kept my distance, our hands barely touching while handing over the stick of gum. I stared out of my window, not wanting her to see the tears in my eyes. Was it finally going to happen, I would be disowned, thrown out of the car, for having sex? Now my baby was going to suffer, too. She didn't want me to have kids. Oh, we'd had similar conversations before.

When I was first married, I visited my parents' house. *Mother stands at the kitchen sink with a skylight over her head, washing lettuce and tomatoes for a salad. She is an attractive fifty-year-old, looking fit from her walks and swims. She has worked in business for the past five years after spending twenty-five years as a homemaker. I stand at the counter across from her. I have long hair, one remnant of my hippie values along with the Birkenstocks on my feet, and am in the middle of graduate school. Michael and I have just gotten married after living together for three years.*

Please don't do that to yourself, Lynn. I want you to experience so many things in life that you'd miss out on if you got pregnant."

Does that mean you really don't want me to have children?" I ask.

Just then her youngest children, Peter and Carrie, aged eleven and fourteen, run through the kitchen and slam the door to the backyard. Carrie yells, "Peter, you give that back. It's Megan's and she's going to kill you."

Mother looks hard at me. "Being a mother is a wonderful thing. But it is so hard to do anything else. I don't want you to waste your talents, your education. I want you to do the things I wish I had done. Think very carefully about what you're doing."

"And I want you to support me in being a mother, Mother. I could do both. Besides, I've already *done a lot of things with my life. I don't know what you mean." Ironic, as her support of my education and career means the world to me.*

After going to the store we went home to the busywork of making dinner and finding a place for me to sleep that night. I took a nap before we ate, creating my own space to be pregnant in, just me and the baby.

Since these conversations we have grown closer, but this closeness does not include sharing our birth experiences. I accept what my mother and I do share instead of trying to reach an agreement or common understanding on the importance of my birth experience. I seek support for my healing journey where I will get it. Peers within the birthing community, support groups and organizations, friends who are open and unthreatened have well filled the gaps.

Support will come from a variety of places and people, not just from one or two sources. Some sources will provide emotional understanding, others will offer practical advice such as how to cope with a fussy baby, and others may offer financial support. The challenge is to accept what is offered and to piece together within oneself a coherent and loving sense of self.

FOR WORK ON YOUR OWN

Question One: How much do I expect total understanding from the people I love? What does it mean to me when my spouse, mother, or friend doesn't agree, changes the subject, or outright doesn't want to listen?

Question Two: How have I sought out support? Was I wise to the pitfalls of looking for it in the wrong places? Have I not sought support because of peoples' initial reactions?

Question Three: How many of my relationships with family, friends, and co-workers have changed since I gave birth? How have they changed?

Question Four: Who can I expect emotional support from? Practical advice? Gifts of time (babysitting, etc.) or money?

FOR FURTHER READING

Duerk, Judith. (1989) *Circle of Stones: Woman's Journey to Herself.* San Diego, CA: LuraMedia.
Gray, Elizabeth Dodson, ed. (1988) *Sacred Dimensions of Women's Experience.* Wellesley, MA: Roundtable Press.
Jones, Carl. (1989) *Sharing Birth: A Father's Guide to Giving Support during Labor.* Westport, CT: Bergin & Garvey.
Lerner, Harriet. (1990) *Dance of Intimacy: A Woman's Guide to Courageous Acts of Change in Key Relationships.* New York: HarperCollins.
Towle, Alexandra, ed. (1988) *Mothers.* New York: Simon & Schuster.

BIRTHING YOURSELF AT THE SAME TIME AS YOUR BABY 4

How a woman was born into the world, physically and emotionally, contributes to how she will give birth to her own baby. When the birthing history between generations is known, information is available to learn from, and then patterns can change. Significant life events can also impact how a baby is born.

Beliefs handed down from mothers or from society to pregnant women that birth is dangerous, unsafe, or undesirable hold power to thwart labor and birth. Though family history and beliefs often appear more solid than stone, they can change, and a woman can break a pattern of family legacy.

Some women are lucky to have rich, empowering messages about birth handed down to them; then, whatever their birth outcomes, those women have strength from which to draw.

During late pregnancy before my first son's birth, I uncovered the first layer of what had already been passed down to me from the previous generation.

One Saturday afternoon in January Mother called out of the blue. "I realized that I am entirely missing my daughter's pregnancy. And this is such a big event, I want to share it with you."

Wow. I get to see my mother!

We had just set the date for a baby shower our neighbors were giving us, and she was invited to come for that weekend in February. I didn't nitpick the fact that she had already seen me pregnant, I was so glad that she wanted to visit.

"But what about your father. Do you want him to come, too?"

Why does she always try and include him? I wanted her all to myself. "Not really. You know how we are together. Tell him it's for

women only." How we are together—what an understatement. I was
still struggling with how to be pregnant around my father. Little had
changed between us since I was a teenager. Most visits included
fights about basic differences: religion, sex, education, the necessity
of violence in the world. I'd learned to not talk with him, so the tension would remain unspoken and unheated. My pregnancy symbol-
ized adulthood, my own family being created, and a belief in life that
I didn't feel safe sharing to much degree with him. I wanted to protect my pregnant belly from the tension that would happen if we
were in the same room together. My mother and father—I wanted to
keep them separate too, didn't want to think of them together.
Mother and I had times of closeness, we could be relaxed when
father wasn't there. I imagined them together when they discovered
they were pregnant with me.

   *The glow of a baby growing in a rosy, warm, nourishing place
where the egg has become fetus, has become baby—but in my
conception and birth, the light is hidden. Mother is so alone in wel-
coming me to earth. Father does his duty, but he is a poor source of
support. Father says, "You've gotten us into a fine mess. Not that I
wasn't involved, I know, I know I was. But if you hadn't followed me
here, if you had only been a little more discreet. Maybe waited until
I contacted you. It's going to be difficult, my parents are upset. Not
that I won't marry you, I will. I want to do the right thing. But Mother
is on her high horse about it, all concerned about what her friends
will think. She'll get over it in time, you've got to give her credit."*

   "Oh dear, what am I going to do? Do you love me, John?"

   *"Of course I love you. I can't help what my mother thinks. She
just assumed that you tricked me, she doesn't understand. I'm willing to face the consequences. The baby'll be all right."*

   The woman, my mother, the woman, me—is molded over time
as a trickster who uses pregnancy to catch a man with her cunning,
and she is forever branded with shame for such behavior. No honor
among women. She will strip her man of any hope for adventure,
fame, satisfaction in life or career, she will wear him down and out
merely by conceiving a baby.

   This history is not just about my own life as the baby who is ill
conceived; it colors beliefs I bring to my pregnancy and to my marriage with Michael. I am afraid he will hate, resent, blame,
denounce, degrade, demean, patronize, revere, and honor in the
name of God for the blessing of a child born from my womb—do all
of these to me when I conceive a baby.

   Ambivalent about being pregnant? Not quite.

   No, I had no idea how to be pregnant around my father.

Mother didn't want to lie and tell him the shower was for women
only, so she handed the dilemma back to me, and I ended up sending him a letter.

Dear Dad,

I was unfair in asking mother to tell you this shower was for
women only, because that isn't true. I'm asking you not to come,
because I'm not feeling real strong these days. As you must also be
aware, whenever we get together there is a lot of conflict and it
would be nice to avoid that right now. I'm hoping you will under-
stand that at this time I would like to share my pregnancy with
Mother. This event is very special for me. I know that you love me,
and I will be stronger after the baby is born. A visit then would work
out better.

I want to thank you for listening to my needs at this time. It
means a lot to me that mother is coming to visit.

He responded by sending with my mother a package of some
toys he picked out for the baby, and a nice card. He stepped aside
and let the women come together around this birth.

Mother came to see me, defying her own family heritage. My
parents were both nineteen years old when she got pregnant. In
1952, they "had to" get married. My paternal grandmother strongly
opposed the marriage, claiming mother had gotten pregnant on purpose to trap father. My maternal grandmother died when my mother
was eight months pregnant, leaving her an angry in-law as her only
maternal support. The doctor would not allow Mother to fly, so she
could not go to her mother's funeral. Father got drunk and hung
over the day of my birth. In a nutshell, that was my entry into the
world.

Catherine, who would be our labor coach, told me how she
got pregnant at eighteen, gave the baby up for adoption, and later
married the father of her child. Fifteen years later she discovered
that both her grandmother and mother got pregnant at eighteen,
both lived apart from the father, then later married the father.
Catherine began to break the pattern by not raising her first child
and not staying married. That intergenerational pattern was
unknown to her until she was thirty-three years old.

Her story scared me. I was afraid to look at my own pregnancy any closer; I felt like a rusty hinge, creaking open to the possibility that I might see yet another reflection of myself in my family, my
past. On the surface I didn't appear to be repeating my parents' pattern at all. I was much older; I had been married for years; this was
a planned pregnancy. All these circumstances proved me different
from my mother.

The similarity that stood out was how bereft my mother was. She had just lost her own mother, was not accepted by her in-laws, and they were living at a poverty level. My father had just joined the air force, and they lived in a basement apartment. I did not want to consider any similarity to myself.

Yet Michael lost a business just before we decided to try getting pregnant, and though I made a good income, we were struggling with debt, no savings, and a sense of loss. Michael began personal bankruptcy proceedings when I was six weeks pregnant. Though we were homeowners and not living in a basement apartment like my parents were, there was still a feeling of poverty. It was not hard to stretch my experience to match hers—perhaps that was even why I had decided to get pregnant in the middle of financial disaster. In addition, though not wanting to consciously grieve over a lack of closeness with my mother, I had been doing just that—had felt pushed away by her for months until her phone call about wanting to visit. I had such a fear of her dying—afraid she would literally repeat the pattern. It was comforting that she had already outlived her mother by eight years, and hopefully she had changed her lifestyle enough to not die so young. My grandmother was only forty-six years old when she died of a stroke. My mother had high blood pressure that was controlled with medication. I prayed that she would take care of herself.

Another similarity was my relationship with my in-laws, which was not exactly close. They did not want to disown me like my mother had been disowned at the time of my birth, but I always felt like a different breed from them. Ginny and Jack had difficulty sharing our successes, like an educational degree or Michael starting a business. They acted as though they did not understand why we did such things. When we told them we were pregnant, they congratulated us, then did not make contact for six months.

In spite of, or perhaps because of all these similarities, at age thirty-four, I felt ready to create my own family. Ironically, by creating this child and new family, my own existence as the child I once was became more real. I was once in a womb as this child was now in my womb. I could not deny its conception or womb-life. I could not deny myself.

Now mother was here to help mend whatever was ailing. This time she flew to be with her own daughter, eight months pregnant. I felt so secure with her in the same room, in the flesh.

She promised to come visit again when the baby was born. After keeping her distance for most of my pregnancy, she was coming through now with flying colors. She must have needed that much time to sort out her new role as grandmother. I was glad she made this visit, glad she had changed.

The morning of the baby shower we all went to the YMCA for a swim. I had on a black maternity swimsuit with ruffles around the legs and top. Mother took my picture in the women's dressing room—"You don't look that big, Lynn. From what you told me I thought you'd look a lot bigger."

"I'm probably still trying to prove to you I'm pregnant by telling you how huge I am."

The next day we sat in the living room with a fire in the wood stove. I was on the couch with my feet up and my head on Michael's shoulder, Mother was in the armchair. I asked her what my birth was like. She said, "The labor was going fine and the doctor asked me, 'Well, dear, this can go on for a few hours or we can get it over with in minutes. What'll it be?' I didn't know any better, I wanted it over. So he used forceps and pulled you right out." Michael got up and went into the kitchen. "It was excruciating. But it didn't last long. And then there you were. You were the only baby born in the hospital that day, Father's Day."

As she talked I had a cringing, aching pain in my groin. I could feel the doctor wrenching me from her body. My vagina contracted instead of loosened as it needed to in order to birth a baby. When I stopped grimacing I said, "I still can't imagine pushing a baby out."

Michael came back into the room saying, "Right, I pinch your thigh and that's labor, as far as we know." Mother changed the subject to my sister Carrie's new apartment, and the mystery of birth settled back in the dust.

We took mother to the airport on a below-zero February day. She had never been so cold—even with a down coat on. On the way, we stopped at an ice sculpture garden and took a picture of her sitting on an ice bench. I enjoyed having California friends and relatives visit Minnesota in the winter. After living in a Mediterranean climate, the shock was amazing. Especially that winter of pregnancy, when I was never cold, walking around outside without a hat, in an unlined corduroy coat. We waved goodbye as she boarded the plane, reassuring her that it rarely got this cold in March, when we would see her again after the baby was born.

That night we lay on the couch together. I was nestled in Michael's arms and the baby was nestled in me. I put Michael's hand on my stomach when the baby was really active, and he talked to it. I rubbed my stomach endlessly, rubbing the baby's back. Welcome to the planet, baby. I thought about my mother's visit and when the baby would meet its grandparents for the first time, and through them, would know its ancestors.

At the time I had no idea of the power of this history. The tightness I felt and the looseness I needed for this first pregnancy and birth were like characteristics of something inanimate and separate like a bolt of cloth, not characteristics of me that needed examination. Even though I had sought out additional resources—massage, a midwife clinic, and all those who would tell me about their births—I did not have, or was not willing to allow, anyone to help me sort out deep fears or identify what the tightness meant.

Only after the birth of my first son was I able to unravel further layers of history and knowledge. I was afraid to be a mother, fearing that being a mother would usurp all other life roles and create despair. I was afraid of the power of birth and what was required of me. The mystery of birth and death hit me smack in the face, and I wanted more mystery at the same time that I was terrified of it. Though this first birth was obviously unpleasant, its power still intoxicated me. I knew that I needed to know more—my heritage, as well as how my own life influenced my giving birth. First I had to forgive myself; blaming myself for what had happened prevented me from accepting how I gave birth and discovering my history.

Three and a half years later, I had forgiven myself and cleared what was needed in order to give birth to my second son, Kyle, in a relatively free, unencumbered way. However, one complication of this clearing was a miscarriage experienced two and a half years after the first birth and shortly before becoming pregnant with Kyle. That loss and experience overshadowed the first birth trauma. The ghost of the miscarried baby, Alice, was at Kyle's birth, both as a loving presence and as a weight of grief.

HOW OTHER LOSSES IMPACT BIRTH

Past loss of a baby pre- or postterm is part of history to be reckoned with. Fear of another death can be present every moment of a pregnancy, and affect a woman's willingness to abandon herself to labor and her baby's emergence. Death of a baby is only touched on here for the issues about a baby's death go beyond the scope of this book. Healing from both birth trauma and infant or fetal death can happen concurrently; the two aspects of birth dovetail one another, yet they are not always one and the same. Similar forms of denial, avoidance of pain, and lack of acceptance of the reality, in this case the dead baby's existence, occur. Speaking out is just as vital. If healing is achieved and a subsequent pregnancy occurs, the mother will have a greater chance of feeling safe and birthing naturally.

If a woman herself was born after a stillborn birth or miscarriage, her own birth may have been shrouded in grief. This history can affect the birth of her own baby, in the scientifically unexplained ways that history repeats itself.

When someone close to the mother has died in recent history—a previous baby, or a mother's sibling or close relative, then death can overshadow the life emerging during birth. Whether grief is deeply buried or fresh and strong, it can be painful to be in the contrasting midst of so powerful a life force as birth.

Only intuitively can a woman know how much of her history, including loss, is involved in the birth of her baby. Attention given to her history clarifies how much heaviness, dread, and avoidance of life are due to her past. Speaking out and grieving openly will alleviate her pain and allow more room for life to take its place.

In my case, the miscarriage strongly impacted my third pregnancy; I was very fearful of another miscarriage. I also still missed the baby I call Alice that died, even while pregnant with another. When Alice's due date arrived, I dreamed I sat on the floor, crying and hugging a large, beautifully patterned womb-shaped urn. I was not ungrateful for the live baby inside of me or for the pregnancy that was now at twenty weeks. I still also had to grieve. After what seemed like endless grieving, by the time labor began, my birthing history had reestablished itself on center stage. But I cannot later tell my VBAC story without first telling the story of Alice's miscarriage.

During the first prenatal exam, the midwife tells me the statistic that one out of five pregnancies end in miscarriage. I don't believe her, because I've only heard of a few, one being my mother's. It's more like one in twenty, I tell myself, it must be an inflated statistic. After trying to get pregnant for over a year with a second child, and already knowing this tiny being inside me, it is too much to know how much risk is involved.

In early October, when I am eleven weeks pregnant, our son's day-care situation falls apart. His teacher is responsible for breaking a child's leg, creating insecurity and fear for our son's safety. My husband Michael and I find him a home day care that is safe, yet the change is stressful. Then Saturday of the same week is the funeral of a friend's brother who died of AIDS. I wonder during the service about being in the presence of death and beginning life in the same moment. A few hours after the service, Michael and I go to a movie starring Gene Wilder about trying to have a baby, and we feel lucky because we're sitting there pregnant. In the theater I begin bleeding, and in a daze realize I could be losing a baby.

Over the next few hours, morning sickness evaporates; food no longer has a tinny taste and there is no more nausea. I call the midwife, who says that I might be miscarrying, and bleeding could continue for awhile before the fetus leaves, or it's possible the bleeding will stop and the baby will be fine. I tell her that it feels dark in my pelvis, that the rosy space is hard to sense now. She pauses, then says that miscarrying women sometimes describe feeling that way. A sinking sensation makes my knees weak.

The bleeding doesn't stop and the next day we go to the clinic, where an ultrasound is done, confirming the baby has died. Now I see an o.b. who gives us the choice between waiting for the baby to leave on its own or having a D & C right away. I choose to wait, wanting to hang onto her, wanting to let my body do its own work.

At 1:00 A.M. I go into labor and after an hour, push out the small sac into the toilet. Then about ten minutes afterwards the placenta slips out, which is the size of my palm. A small birth for a small baby; I realize this really was a baby, and losing a baby includes a birth. Despair hits first, and that night I dream of falling down black steps into an unknown world.

An empty space is being created not from desperation, though that is also within me. No, the desperate space is a void, a black hole that can suck you into an endless head spin. Empty is not a void, or evil, or black quicksand, it is space. Sit in the emptiness, let it be. Empty stomach, empty arms, empty mind, empty— allows spirit to speak, a clear sensation as though a wind flows freely. I wake up and realize I can hear spirit when empty. At the same time I reel from the loss, and we go about our grieving as though she were an integral part of our family, which she is.

A dragon waits in the empty space, swishes his tail back and forth, creating a swath that wipes through my parents' old bedroom on Pomona Street. Where my mother had a miscarriage that no one ever talked about. Where they tried for more babies, though no one ever mentioned wanting more children. Tried for ten years. The dragon is my companion as I am caught in my family's miseries. The misery of children, of trying to have a baby and failing. The green bedspread with brown piping is at the center of the scene with my mother lying on it, saying she had a miscarriage and, "Please go away, I want to be left alone." Yes, so I and my brother go away to the family room and never is another word said. How much of that event twenty-five years ago am I still carrying around?

We find a tiny white embroidered pillow in which to place her body, and bury her in a field of tall, wild prairie grass surrounded by cottonwood trees. The mantra I say over and over is, Alice, you will be missed, please come back soon, we love you.

Empty is the space between the stars. When Alice died, she went far away out in the universe to live on a star. I go to visit sometimes, and the visit is empty, echoing sounds and sights in space, yet comforting. Alice, you left me empty, I wish you hadn't. Yet you are part of the emptiness. So how can that be all bad?

Later that day many friends come to our house for a ceremony to say good-by both to Alice and all our dreams of her, then we have potluck. Four families bring squash dishes, and two apple desserts complete a very fall meal. The sharp pangs of grief are partly absorbed by this day, as memories are created of ceremony as well as pain.

In my own need for making the situation real, I tell people I've lost a baby. Only then do I begin hearing of other miscarriages. "Oh, I'm sorry to hear this, I had two miscarriages, between my two children." Then a note from a friend in a dance class describes a stillborn baby at five months. Then another woman confides of three miscarriages before birthing a baby daughter after switching doctors and discovering a treatable thyroid problem. As though the floodgates have opened up I hear many stories, many losses. I begin to believe the midwife's statistic, and shift my perspective so that a woman who does not experience a miscarriage or loss related to fertility or birth is unusual.

One night I take Michael to the emergency room after he has fallen down the basement stairs and broken his ankle. I stand next to his wheelchair, and a nurse comes up to me and asks when I'm due. "I'm not pregnant," I say. "I had a miscarriage three weeks ago." The nurse says with a small smile, "Oh, I thought I saw a little bulge," and wheels Michael away. I affirm, I am empty. Other women are full with child. I am empty, the opposite. To say the affirmation keeps me sane when I see women pregnant or with babies. They are full. It keeps me sane when someone mistakes me for being pregnant.

During the follow-up exam the o.b. tells us to wait three months before conceiving again. With our track record, conceiving on demand is a pipe dream, and besides, I need to affirm life, go toward the direction of life. Michael wants to wait as the doctor suggests, and that night we have a rational conversation about what good advice it is, that time to heal emotionally and physically is necessary, and there is plenty of time for another baby. I agree with him to wait, then we quietly walk upstairs and have entirely unprotected sex, our hearts winning over our minds.

My advent this year as the holidays approach is to sit with empty, trusting that the future will be full, or part of the future will be. For empty is now firmly rooted inside, has a place, and encroaches on my heart, requiring it to open, and requiring breath to travel and affirm life down to my pubic bone and beyond. Breath in empty is unheeded, flows easily.

Three months go by anyway, but trying to conceive helps me cope with the grief, and with the empty space. In January we succeed, and I am thankful to not go through our usual year of efforts. Yet the miscarriage is so recent, I am gripped with fear of another one happening, and so the joy of a new life full of light and creation exists side by side with the fear of death and loss. I know this new baby is not Alice, because I see her clearly on her star, far away. But Alice's presence is felt throughout the pregnancy, especially around her due date, and the last trimester. She is a midwife to my second son's birth, who is born the day before the anniversary of her death.

The pregnancy with my second son, Kyle, included a combination of tending to the remnants of fear, anger, and grief over the first birth and tending to the grief over the miscarriage. I believe Alice truly was a midwife to Kyle's birth. When I had labored with her, though she was a fraction the size of a full-term baby, it was the first time I had ever pushed a baby out; she taught me that valuable lesson. As Kyle moved down the birth canal, Alice cheered. I imagine they knew each other out in the stars, and she may be his guardian angel. Or my guardian angel.

Acknowledging past losses loosens up one's insides and makes a woman whole. All parts of her are present, and fear of the past, of pain, of the unknown become more defined, diminished, and less threatening. Grief is part of life and is an aspect of birth not acknowledged enough. Death is always present at birth; the door between death and life cracks open as the new baby emerges. The sense of a woman's own death or her baby's is the other side of the coin from birth. When a baby arrives, the potential for its loss is also born; an ever-present reminder that life includes death.

HISTORY OF ABUSE

Because birth is a powerful life-affirming event, a history of abuse—the opposite of life affirmation, creates a complex situation. After abuse, a woman constricts and insulates herself for protection.

Yet birthing requires her to be open and vulnerable. Sexual abuse, in particular, elicits a closed, protective, mute, distrustful stance. If the abuse happened in childhood, this stance is a longtime pattern, so ingrained a woman might not be consciously aware of it. She has body memories that contribute to her pushing away life, but once memories are unlocked, her energy is able to flow through her. Acknowledging abuse in her background and finding ways to protect herself other than shutting down are fundamental tools she can use to heal herself and to increase her potential to give birth without intervention.

Though there is scant written material about this connection, many midwives, obstetricians, and other healers are aware of the relationship between a history of abuse and the diagnosis of dystocia (failure of labor to progress), resulting in cesareans or major interventions. Often dystocia is attributed to the large size of the baby or the small size of the mother. However, one obstetrician described the situation when sexual abuse was part of a woman's history as "brain dystocia," meaning that something is going on inside the woman's head that does not allow labor to progress. Once the memories or emotions have been addressed, a woman has the potential to succeed in opening and pushing out her baby.

This was true for Marybeth. Her first baby had been born cesarean due to failure to progress after forty-eight hours of labor. When her daughter Rose was a year old, Marybeth realized she had been sexually abused by her father. She became aware of incidents in late childhood, age nine and up. When she became pregnant again, her midwife referred her to therapy about the abuse, hoping to increase her chances of an uncomplicated delivery, thus not repeating the pattern of the first birth. Marybeth became confident that having acknowledged the abuse and carefully chosen her caregivers, she had cleared the way for a successful labor.

One action step Marybeth took as a result of the therapy had to do with her mother. They were on good terms, with Marybeth being as honest as she could be about her current situation. She had not yet felt any anger toward her mother for not preventing the sexual abuse. Her mother had been invited to be present at the baby's birth and had already bought a plane ticket to join Marybeth a week before her due date. She planned to stay a month. Yet Marybeth was uncomfortable with her mother's projected presence at the birth.

> I called her a month ahead, and said, "Mom, I can't have you at the birth. It's just not working." I didn't know why, I didn't know all of it, I just knew it. And I honored that, and she heard it, it was really hard for her, and she said, "My tickets are already bought, why

don't I come and just hang out?" She got here, she came a week and a half early.

Five days after my due date I went into labor, mild at first. I started having back pain, contractions got heavier, just like it had happened the first time. That's when we called the midwives. After what happened during my first birth, and then realizing the sexual abuse, I wanted nothing to do with the hospital, and the midwives were great.

I couldn't eat anything, I'd throw up each time I tried, but this time I knew that wasn't a serious sign. The midwives came by, checked me, I was only one centimeter. But they were so confident that I could do this. We did another twenty-four hours of back labor, frequent contractions, I was still one centimeter.

By now two days had gone by, and the midwives said I needed to rest, and that I might need morphine. What other alternative was there? I didn't want to start out with drugs, it would have been like dominoes for me, I'd end up exactly where I was the first time. Then they thought of doing hypnosis, and called someone they knew. So my husband Henry put me in the car and drove me across town to this doctor's office who was seeing me on her lunch hour. I came out an hour later, transformed.

I realized in that session that I had thought the abuse had started at age nine, well, it started more like age three, and there had been penetration. I started to see how I closed my heart at that time, but I didn't just close my heart to Dad, I closed it to Mom. This labor was stopped because of my heart being closed, as well as there being a penis in the way, so that I literally couldn't open and give birth to the child. But it was mostly about my heart being closed.

At the end of the hypnosis session these words came out of me, she didn't tell me what to say, this came on my very own. She said, "What do you need to do now to be able to birth this child?"

I said I need to open my heart.

"To who?"

"Dad, Mom, and Henry."

"And maybe the child?" she asked, and I said yes. And I meant my first child, Rose, and I meant the new baby. And then I knew I needed to open my heart to myself. I wasn't even allowing my own self in my own heart. I walked through all that and it was hard, some of the hardest stuff I've ever done. That doctor was so positive about the healing potential.

Then we went back home and I was really tired, but the nature of the contractions had changed. The midwives told me that I would have to put the information I just learned on the back burner and return to it after the birth. So I listened to the tape once more, and I cried and cried, and then I put the tape away. The midwives did an enema, and that made the back labor much easier. I was able to relax, but not sleep. Then stuff the midwives had tried for the past two days that hadn't worked, began to work. Guided imagery, walking around.

I realized I was feeling pressure with my mother just being in the area, after what happened with the hypnosis. I called her up and said, "Mom, won't you go to Wisconsin to visit friends? I feel too much pressure. I hear you say, hurry up, I only have two more weeks to be with you, hurry up and have the baby." So she agreed to go to Wisconsin until I invited her back, and I didn't know when that would be. I didn't exactly know what that was all about, but I am just so glad that I honored that. It was the hardest thing that I have ever done, to call her again and say, "I can't have you here."

Then I was able to keep some food down. By the next morning, there were stronger contractions, things began kicking in, I was at three and a half centimeters. This is day three now. The bag of waters was in front of the baby's head acting as a cushion. They broke the bag, and in half an hour I was four more centimeters dilated. Then we were on home stretch. I was in the bathtub, and could feel the head in the vagina, so I got out of the tub. My friend Kathy had been taking care of Rose, and she brought her over to be with us. I started out on all fours to push, but ended up squatting against Henry. Then my second daughter was born, she came out healthy, I had just a little tear. It was so wonderful to be at home and to have her safe and healthy, and to have all of us together.

I couldn't have opened up in the hospital, there would have been no hypnosis, and they wouldn't have let me labor for three days like I did. The first two days of birth being so slow was such a powerful thing, it allowed me to get to the bottom of the barrel. The midwives knew I could do it.

Mom showed up the day after the birth, and all she did for two weeks was clean up after the birth and cook for us for two weeks.

As I started to work on this birth situation and the sexual abuse, I realized that not only could I not let Mom into my heart, but my bottom line is I was scared I was going to die. At some point my spirit did die. I just shut my heart out and my spirit died. It's hard to understand when, or why or how, and I still don't, just that somewhere I died. And I see the same patterns throughout my whole life until now. Rose's birth added another layer, it didn't open me up, not until now. Not that having her hasn't helped, it has. I love her so much, but now it's even better. Her birth helped me see that I needed to do things differently.

I haven't gone through a lot of anger at Mom yet. I was angry at Dad for awhile, but not even very big-time with him, I suspect that's still coming. I was angry at Henry for three years. And that's where I was expressing it, I was inappropriate with it at times, because it was the first time I was ever angry in twenty-eight years. And all of a sudden he got the brunt of it. I think it's not just the abuse, there's this other stuff with Mom not being there for me. It's the abuse, but not the sexual abuse specifically. I didn't realize that until this birth.

There is so much to bite off from the hypnosis. So much came up, and I haven't listened to the tape again yet. Maybe birth is a sort of passage to let go of all this sexual abuse stuff, because I found out there's more than just the abuse that created who I am today. All this stuff with Mom, and fear of dying, and all that stuff is related, but it's more than the abuse with Dad, it's another whole ball game. It alleviated all that pressure, how I was screwed up because of my Dad and this abuse. I held onto that for so long and used it as a curtain.

Now I have this base, I have a feeling of satisfaction that is totally different from the first birth. My reality is different, and I get to draw from birth all this strength that I discovered. That's the other side of the coin, I am so grateful I got to have this side, too. Two years from now I'll discover things, keep on drawing from that place. It's a different path. I would walk out of a hospital now, I wouldn't tolerate anything like I did before.

What happened to Marybeth during those three days of labor was a compression of what often takes others several years. However, two things stand out that can be true for every woman. One is that birth is such a powerful experience, with so much potential for openness and growth, that it can be this strong a catalyst for any individual. The other component is that Marybeth did a lot of work ahead of time to optimize her chances for the second birth to happen the way it did. She chose caregivers who would support this kind of effort, and she had developed her own physical and emotional strength from which to draw during the birth. Additionally, Marybeth was consciously aware of her history with her parents and its immediate influence on how she was giving birth.

Much of the healing described here occurs after a cesarean or major interventions due to dystocia or another vaguely defined reason. When abuse has occurred and is unacknowledged, any way to give birth without opening, without giving up the protection and shell the woman desperately needs, will be sought on an unconscious level. A cesarean is a way out in this case—a way for the baby to leave the woman's body without her becoming sexually vulnerable. The woman still faces the healing challenge of finding the inner power that will allow her to learn to open and be vulnerable. In unlocking her anger, fear, grief, and rage, she ultimately leads herself to effective self-protection and joy.

Any birth is powerful. Even with unforeseen medical interventions, planned medical interventions, or unexpected loss, potential for healing is present. Days, months, or many years after a birth, a woman can tap into this power and weave her own tapestry of healing from abuse. Her personal cycle of repeating the abuse pattern within herself or with her family will be transformed.

RELIVING ONE'S OWN BIRTH

Before a woman gives birth, her only personal experience to draw upon is her own birth into the world. The argument is made that it is impossible to remember when one was so young or when one was alive in the womb. Rebirthers would disagree. Some hypnotists and body therapists would disagree. People who have early memories of those times would also disagree. Even if those memories are held within the body without words or images, the presence of those memories may guide a woman through labor.

Not only is a woman influenced by prenatal emotional or environmental patterns, her actual birth journey out of her own mother's womb may be reenacted. In my case, I did not seek out a birthing memory, but one spontaneously came to me.

> When Evan, my first child, was fourteen months old, my massage therapist and former labor coach, Catherine, reminded me that during pregnancy I was too busy to do the work she saw most women do, that of clearing trauma from their own births. My struggle had been primarily with work issues. She thought that was what was going on now. Maybe it was the power of suggestion, maybe I was just ready to do what she mentioned. But soon after, one day while she gave me a massage, I had a vivid memory of being born. *I am pulled out of my mother's body, can feel the forceps. After emerging, my legs and feet flap in the wind like a dishtowel hanging on a clothesline. The doctor's hands wave me around in a room that is lighted yet has deep shadows. A linoleum table top looms toward me and I am splatted onto it. I want to be close to my mother. And I*

don't know what to do with my legs.

As my senses returned to the massage room, my body was curled up in a ball, my hands were numb and turned inward at the wrists, my legs were numb, I had trouble breathing, and my face was all pinched.

"What happened, Lynn?" Catherine asked, holding the soles of my feet as they slowly uncurled.

"I think I just saw my own birth."

"Oh, you had a little spontaneous rebirthing," Catherine calmly said, as though she saw this kind of thing happen every day. She gave me the name of a rebirther, someone who works with a breathing technique to help people clear out birth trauma like I was having. My discomfort was great enough I was willing to try it.

Mary was the rebirther's name. I liked her, which helped me feel more comfortable while lying on a mat on the floor with my face all pinched and scrunched as she watched. I breathed like she told me to, in and out without holding the breath. It came easily. Soon my temples got very tight and throbbed. *My whole body tingles and at the same time becomes rigid. My hands curl inward, my jaw moves on its own, one cheek moves independently from the other, the mouth puckers. My stomach and thighs are weighted down as though there are metal free weights placed on them. My eyes open to make sure Mary isn't sitting on me—she isn't, but that is how heavy the sensation feels. She suggests moving my legs if I want to. As soon as they move I want to kick hard, and then the heavy feeling in my thighs lessens. Mary has me turn so I can push against the wall. I curl up, then uncurl as I push, arching my back as my legs straighten. I am pushing myself out of the womb for the first time. The pain in my temples is from the forceps. I see red and feel rage at that doctor for not letting me push myself out. I am shocked about not knowing this is how babies are born. Of course! Babies are doing their part, they push against the womb. Sensation begins to return in my legs all the way down to my feet, though the feeling is still faint. The warm birth canal is secure around me as my head and then body move slowly out, moving to the rhythm of many heartbeats, my body undulating, arcing like a fish jumping.*

I woke up from that journey relieved, focused on my own birth, not Evan's. Now I knew how to push a baby out, because I knew how to push myself out.

I have difficulty describing this experience any more clearly; the results were that my body knew how to push out a baby, whereas before it had no idea how to push out a baby. Or perhaps the memory of how to give birth was activated from some form of collective memory. Another helpful aspect of reliving my own birth was that I was able to separate this influence from what happened during my first son's birth. I was more forgiving of myself and of him for being born in a traumatic situation. Shortly after this rebirthing, when my first child, Evan, was one and a half years old, I dreamed:

> *I stand in an empty room and an operating table is wheeled in. Green sheets cover a pad, there are metal springs and clamps along its sides. I put my hands on the operating table and remember. I remember Evan being born, and say thank you. That operating room hummed with birth. They did their jobs well, witnessed a new life amongst sterility. They revered his life, handled him gently, resuscitated him with all the technology available. Bless every person in that room.*
>
> Bless all healers who touch a pregnant woman. Bless their hands, their knowledge, their wisdom. Bless their eyes that witness so many births.

The point of remembering and learning history is to give birth events more respect and to allow the healing forces to flow through a new mother in whatever form she needs or wants. Every new mother deserves to glow with the force and light only being in the presence of a brand new life can create.

FOR WORK ON YOUR OWN

Question One: What is the history of birth in your family? What was your birth like? Ask your mother, grandmother, aunts, sisters, or anyone else who may have information about your birth, siblings' births, and their own births. Include both the physical event and what the parents' lives were like at the time of birth. Record their stories in some way, with a journal or a tape recorder.

If relatives are not able or willing to talk with you—if you are adopted or others have died or refuse to discuss birth, then other methods are necessary. In this case, pretend your mother, grandmother, or siblings are relating your birth story and theirs. Pretend you know what happened, what these births were like, and write down your pretend memories. These stories also are useful, informative, and true.

Question Two: Reflect on your personal history since you were born; are there any events that stand out in significance that could have influenced how you gave birth, or felt about giving birth?

FOR FURTHER READING

Forward, Susan. (1989) *Toxic Parents: Overcoming Their Hurtful Legacy and Reclaiming Your Life*. New York: Bantam Books.

Kasl, Charlotte Davis. (1989) *Women, Sex, and Addiction: A Search for Love and Power*. New York: Ticknor & Fields.

Miller, Alice. (1984) *Thou Shalt Not Be Aware*. New York: Meridian/Penguin.

Panuthos, Claudia. (1984) *Transformation through Birth*. Westport, CT: Bergin & Garvey.

Peterson, Gayle. (1991) *An Easier Childbirth: A Workbook for Pregnant Women*. Los Angeles: Jeremy Tarcher Press.

Ray, Sondra. (1986) *Ideal Birth*. Berkeley, CA: Celestial Arts.

Orr, Leonard, and Ray, Sondra. (1978) *Rebirthing in the New Age*. Berkeley, CA: Celestial Arts.

Sanford, Linda. (1990) *Strong at the Broken Places*. New York: Random House.

Simkin, Penny. (1992) "Overcoming the Legacy of Childhood Sexual Abuse: The Role of Caregivers and Childbirth Educators. *Birth Journal: Issues in Perinatal Care 19*. Cambridge, MA: Scientific Publications. (To date, the only information in print about the relationship between sexual abuse and the experience of labor and birth.)

POST-BABY TRANSFORMATION: YOU ARE UNEXPECTEDLY CATAPULTED TO ANOTHER PLANET

5

When a new baby is brought home, it acts as a catalyst for a wonderful transformation as a family is expanded and remade. The family as it once was is gone forever; a new face is at the kitchen table, changing everyone's relationships.

My own sense of control over daily events was also gone forever. Every room in the house had evidence of a baby; a swing, bouncy seat, extra diapers, clothes, and blankets were now living room fixtures. My own physical appearance included spit-up marks on clothes, dark circles under my eyes, and large breasts. My marriage was forever changed; we hired our first sitter when Evan was eight months old, implying one of us was always with him, and we were rarely only a couple. My career was also forever changed, as I began the precarious balancing act between motherhood and work.

When my first baby was a week old I dreamed that *I am driving in the parking lot at work, not able to find a space. There is shampoo in my hair as I didn't have time to rinse it out. I arrive at the office on the fourth floor and walls are being knocked down and moved, the files are totally rearranged so that I cannot find anything, including my paycheck.* I woke up laughing and crying.

I told mother my dream when she brought breakfast up on a tray. While sitting in the rocker nursing Evan, I cried, so worried about work. How would we manage, where were we going to come up with the money to live on while I could not work? Being so vulnerable, the street felt only a step away, and I was afraid of ending up homeless or on welfare. First we would lose our house and live in a cheap apartment, then we wouldn't be able to afford day care and our jobs wouldn't work out, and then we'd be homeless.

Mother was reassuring. She convinced me that at least for the next couple of weeks since I couldn't work anyway, why not focus on myself and the baby. I could worry all I wanted to next month. Michael walked into the bedroom with a cup of coffee. He sat down on the floor next to the rocker and listened to our conversation, then pushed me further. "Pretend you resigned from your job, you've retired. Pretend you're not going back to work at all."

At first I looked at him dumbfounded. "Are you serious?" Well, why not trust him? The idea was beautiful, it had appeal and relief. I was incapacitated to the point where I could agree that I was better off doing what mother and Michael suggested. "Well, okay. At least for the next week I know I'm not going anywhere."

"I wish you'd give yourself a break, Lynn." Michael said as he took Evan who finished the first breast from my lap to change him. "Come on, you little poopmaster general, let's get you cleaned up." He laid Evan on our bed on a changing pad, lifted up his long legs and made them do bicycling motions. With Evan in a clean diaper, Michael held him on his chest, kissed his head at least ten times, then handed him back to me, my arms ready to feel his body again.

I relaxed, at least for hours at a time. Then I would slip and say something like, "I could go back and just do my groups at first, I'd only be gone a few hours—"

And Michael would say, "Remember, you've retired. You don't have to work. Relax, put your feet up."

"But what about—"

"Lynn, drop it. You're not going anywhere. Take a break." I noticed my unwashed hair, feeling tired after getting up at least twice in the night, my stomach still big and sore, and how I would not let Evan out of my sight for longer than twenty minutes. I'd slow down for a moment and recognize that Michael was showing me that he had trust in our future, and trust that he would pick up the slack that I was rapidly creating. He encouraged me to take care of myself and be with Evan, and voiced his frustration when I talked about going back to work full-time. "I don't know how to convince you that's not necessary. I want you to believe me."

"You're right, I can barely walk around the block. I need more time." Michael gave me a hug, held my hand with his fingers twined in mine, and kissed me on my cheek and lips. He went out of the room to do the laundry and talk with my mother about plans for dinner. I tried to hang onto the secure feeling just occurring, but unfortunately it would begin slipping away as soon as he left the room.

Nothing could have prepared me for the reality of a new baby. I was also unprepared for how motherhood would impact my career.

Even with familial and societal support, this transition is difficult. Without support, it feels overwhelming and unbearable. My loyalties were now divided. The intensity of attachment to and responsibility for the baby is unfortunately juxtaposed with the pressures of career or work. Financial considerations are more pronounced as baby-related costs arise. Amidst this adjustment or transformation, the wondrous experience of new parenthood deserves attention. Whether attention is given depends on attitudes and resources.

I had experienced close attachments in my life, but nothing compared with this new baby. I now understood that I would easily run in front of a bus to push my child to safety; it would not be so easy to know this about anyone else. This bond was all the more threatening after a difficult birth; I had reason to fear losing him. Plus, the more I grew to love him, the more I had to lose, requiring the deepest letting go of my life.

I became one of those parents at a party that could talk about baby details for hours, and I saw the world—everything in the world—through the metaphor of birth. Everyone was on a birth journey of some sort, and every challenge was the challenge of birth. Like a war hero turning a household into a battlefield with soldiers, I turned all parts of my life into a birth drama. Especially the first few months, when the baby was so tiny, I could not go an hour without thinking of him and viewing everyone else in relation to him. I was especially preoccupied when I went back to work after five weeks.

After nursing Evan, I'd pull together my dishevelled business clothes, put the breast pads back in place, and drive to the office. By now my office hours were increased to three full days a week, plus early Thursday morning staff meetings. I wore professional clothes, which felt cramped as my breasts leaked and demanded I feed my baby. A "normal" performance was required, normal meaning completely involved as a psychologist, able to discuss theories and clients, and pretending those details mattered to me. I pretended to be normal, yet would not deny what my body told me while seated at the conference table. I was still swollen and voluptuous, and still had a stomach on me, from surgery and pregnancy. Strangers probably thought I *was* pregnant. I automatically filled out forms, took notes, submitted expenses, discussed business and cases; inside me baby visions squeezed everything else out to the edges. The weight of him in my arms could be felt and his face could be seen no matter what I was doing. His pout—his rosebud, full lower lip relaxed and moist after nursing as he sat in his infant seat, was a vivid memory.

"Lynn, are you going to the conference on multiple personality case management?" No, thank you. Let other people keep such wheels greased, I would coast as long as possible. Besides, talk about multiple personalities, I was struggling with two of my own— my home persona and my work persona. I thought to myself:

Where are the conferences on birth psychology, how giving birth transforms a woman's life like nothing else? And what does this mean, postpartum depression? So clinical, could they just give me antidepressants and take care of this? No way this is depression. This is major league change. Come on, most of the people in this room have either given birth or witnessed it. All of them have been born. Tell me what you think I'm going through. Let's put a six-week old baby on the middle of this conference table and see how everyone responds. What if just once a month only one child to every twenty adults were brought to the "workplace" for a visit. What wonderful chaos would reign. Isn't that why most of us are working? We have families to support and love, children to raise, relate to, and enjoy. Multiple personalities spring from not being loved as a child, from horrible abuse. Let's get personal here. I just gave birth, and it matters, damn it. Even if you don't talk about birth, my work is going to change because of it.

I had to hide motherhood at the office, be discrete about pumping milk. No one knew what my body had been through except for the absence of a big stomach. No one knew how Evan was born unless I chose to tell them. The mystery of birth was shrouded at the office.

Waiting for the elevator at the end of the day, my breasts throbbed with milk, Evan's delayed six o'clock feeding. I couldn't make casual hallway conversation about my new motherlife that took up my mind's and body's attention. "My breasts are so full I can't wait to get home and nurse," wasn't like talking about the weather or noticing someone's new outfit.

Clients asked about the new baby, and then the work went on. As it was supposed to. I was there to work, which by itself did not bother me. I liked what I did. I just wanted to be a mother more than I wanted to be at the office.

At home was this tiny baby who suckled my breast, who had sweet-milk breath. He was small enough to fit in the white wicker bassinet, part of my dream of being a new mother. I completely surrounded him with soft blankets and cotton padding. When eating dinner, we pulled the bassinet up to the table so we could look at Evan. We gazed at his little body enclosed in a drawstring gown and swaddled in a receiving blanket; he radiated light, warm breath came out of his rosy mouth. His eyelids were transparent and delicate; when he opened them his blue eyes melted my insides. We both had irresistible urges to hold him, and he spent hours sleeping in my arms or Michael's. We didn't want to let go.

I took long walks with Evan in his stroller. Our house is near a lake with a three-mile circumference. The diaper bag would be loaded with my lunch and his diapers, and we would be gone for as long as we wanted. We would stop to breast-feed him under a blanket whenever he got hungry, while watching the lake and the birds. Summer arrived and I began to wear a bathing suit under my clothes so that if he fell asleep I could sunbathe. The scar became toughened by the sun, stretched from swimming. The sun shone on us, healing whatever was ailing. We walked home through different neighborhoods, stopping at a deli or a used clothing store, stopping at a park to watch older kids. I couldn't imagine him running or swinging—that was still a lifetime away. We would arrive home in the late afternoon in time to give him a bath, fold the laundry. My hands touched baby skin and clean, soft, tiny clothes. I gently patted him dry with his baby towel.

I am among many new mothers who will never forget what it was like to return to work and leave a new baby with someone else. This adjustment is frequently disregarded, yet another aspect of birth that is denied or minimized. It is no wonder that many women experience depression after birth.

In retrospect, having work to take my mind off of trauma may have been a blessing. If I had been more isolated, more opportunity would have existed for rumination and self-blame. For women who plan to stay at home and had tumultuous births, the isolation is a real danger.

I was fortunate to bond so deeply with my first son after having had such a traumatic birth. Breast-feeding nurtured that bond, as well as the inherent desire to have children. Unbearable aspects of being out of balance in regard to career and home became bearable because of the adoration I felt. Other new mothers respond differently; their feelings toward a new baby reflect their pain, rage, and avoidance. Bonding is not always a given. As previously mentioned, it took Judy many months to bond with her daughter as a result, she believes, of having had her by cesarean. With a less than solid mother-baby relationship, adjusting to this new life is even more difficult.

Lack of bonding may be the result of a traumatic birth. It may also reflect a history of abuse; with the baby's arrival, the mother's own childhood history is more easily accessed. This aspect of postpartum adjustment is beyond the scope of this book. However, since birth trauma is related to postpartum adjustment, as discussed in the following section, parallels can be made. Also refer to chapter 4, "Birthing Yourself at the Same Time as Your Baby." There, the relationship between past abuse and the nature of labor and birth is more comprehensively discussed. The adjustment after a baby arrives is a natural extension of this entire issue.

POSTPARTUM DEPRESSION REDEFINED

A woman's birth, if empowering and affirming, lingers on in her awareness, strengthening her through the first months of new motherhood and fueling her sense of ability to handle strenuous challenges. The warm glow of new life still surrounds her, no matter what kind of bedlam condition the living room is in.

After the vaginal, natural birth of my second child, I kept looking around me wide-eyed at the absence of trauma. I was overjoyed at being able to focus on the baby and feeling the glow from accomplishing the birth with my own power. I was able to gage how much of the postpartum adjustment was that alone, and not adjustment due to birth trauma. I knew that I was delirious from lack of sleep and learning how to juggle the care of two children, and not delirious or "overreacting" about how my baby was born. He was born, simply. Yes, I tore a bit and had three stitches, there was meconium but no lasting effects, I had a hemorrhoid. If I really tried, I could complain or be depressed, but I had no need. This time I could roar if I wished, instead of be mute with pain. I was able to jump fully into the tasks of new motherhood and coping with two children—which was plenty. No doubt adjustment was required.

After a baby arrives, a new mother is challenged for various reasons. She relives her own childhood through her children. She must discover how to nurture herself as well as her baby in all ways—physically, mentally, emotionally, spiritually. She faces decisions about how to direct her passion, whether to parcel it out between home life and work. Is she well suited to being with children twenty-four hours a day? All these issues and more come to a head when the baby comes, no matter how it arrives. What a surprise when the baby pokes his or her little head out from the womb, looks around, and basically says, "Hello, please feed me, comfort me, and entertain me every moment," and, "from now on."

It takes a lot of faith and courage to do this job. After my first baby, I had great respect for any woman who had given birth intentionally more than once. To take on the enormous work load and dedication, for the many years it takes to raise a child—the feeding and clothing alone—boggled my mind.

With the challenges of recovering from trauma in addition to this new parenting lifestyle, many new mothers do not cope as well with reality. There is the by now familiar chant, "What is important is you have a healthy baby; put the past behind you now, you've got to think about what is ahead." At this critical time when her new life is truly starting, the mother feels bereft, and confused with these new challenges. A piece of her is dead, and she does not know if it will ever come alive again.

The same pattern of denial exists for the postbaby adjustment; many new mothers are overwhelmed and scared about their daily lives. Yet remarks often relayed include: "Can you imagine, my mother had six." "Wait until you have another one, two children is when you really become a full-time parent." "Women have been having babies for millions of years." "You can handle it, everybody makes it through this first year."

I am sure my own reactions were strong due to the nature of Evan's birth; I had a lot of trauma to recover from. However, I was not unusual. I certainly tried to rationalize every bit of difficulty. I felt guilty for not enjoying this new baby every minute. I berated myself for being overwhelmed. I felt anger and humiliation, and tried to figure out how I caused a prolapsed cord and cesarean operation. I wanted to tell everyone what happened and at the same time wanted no one to know what happened.

Another common trap used to minimize a woman's own birth issues is to compare experiences. After Ellen's first birth, before she unleashed her authority, she said,

> I didn't have it so bad, there was no infection. We planned the birth well, and I didn't have a cesarean—when Jason was taken from me, my husband was always with him. I have a lot to be thankful for. Mary's birth was much worse, have you heard what happened to her? Now there's someone who really needs help.

Comparisons are rarely helpful. They are either a way to deny one's own pain because it isn't as bad as someone else's, or a way to put oneself down because the situation is worse than another's. Comparisons do not accept or acknowledge differences; they catapult observations into judgments. Once more, regardless of others' experiences or opinions, if a woman feels bereft, traumatized, angry, griefstricken, disappointed, or self-doubting, then she deserves to pay attention to what is happening. She deserves care and understanding, which will aid her navigation through these beginning phases of motherhood, and she will learn how to heal herself.

Much of postpartum depression, from the perspective of recovering from unexpected outcomes, is about the necessity to heal. Since a woman's experience can be minimized in so many ways, it is easy to believe that the pain is in her head and that she has no reason to feel disappointed or angry or scared. The most useful and accurate definition of depression I know is that it is anger turned inward. When a woman minimizes or denies, that is exactly what occurs. Anger is directed inside, or stuffed to a far corner inside oneself, rather than expressed outwardly.

The term postpartum depression is simply depression occurring during the postpartum period. Rather than there being something magical about this term, it is only the defining of depression at a specific time.

I do not deny the importance or overwhelming nature of the adjustment required to care for a new infant, nor the effect of high levels of hormones present after birth. But bouts of crying can also be a release, not always a symptom of depression. Some women experience a new infant with joy and excitement; there is the potential for a high rather than a low. Some researchers hypothesize this as an individual's varying response to hormone levels. However, if the depression is related to unexpected birth outcomes, I believe that then addressing them in that context will help.

Ellen, who gave birth to her first baby vaginally but with many interventions, told her doctor at the six-week checkup that she was upset about having had the vacuum extraction.

I didn't realize that I was upset about all the other interventions yet. The doctor told me that the vacuum extraction happened because I had a nine and a half pound baby, and subsequent babies are often bigger, so I'd better get used to it. So then I planned on during my next pregnancy to not gain so much weight, and try to make a smaller baby. Plus he was ten days late, maybe the next one would be on time, and not so big. As though I could control the size of my baby.

I thought I had done such a good job of preparing. I had chosen a female doctor, I had gone over my birth plan with her, I had gone over it with the nurse when we arrived at the hospital. Maybe if I had taped it to my door it would have made a difference. But my birth plan failed except for avoiding a cesarean, and I always thought that at least that didn't happen. But that's a way I minimize what happened to me. All those people telling me what a wonderful big baby I had, and then following that with horror stories of their own. One woman I knew kept telling me how she almost *died* giving birth, she almost *died*. So what could I say to her? I said nothing. I knew I didn't feel good, but I didn't know why.

Ellen was told that the reason for the intervention was her baby's size. The lack of acknowledgment of the loss she felt about her birth experience contributed to her sense of failure. Her anger was indeed turned inward and transformed into numbness and depression. As she searched out more education, exercised her ability to make her own decisions, and decided to say what she needed to say, her anger was directed outward, where it belonged.

Vicky's adjustment to a new baby was almost entirely overshadowed by her birth experience. After an unnecessary cesarean leaving her with a sense of violation, she felt rage and despair. Vicky was adamant that whatever depression she felt was due to the birth.

Postpartum depression? I don't think I ever had postpartum depression, I had posttraumatic depression. I don't think I would have ever had any kind of depression at all if what had happened to me didn't happen. I've often wondered if people weren't depressed after the birth because of what happened during their birth. If they don't realize that they've been raped, and cut up, and all this stuff. Because I don't think postpartum depression is being depressed because the baby had come out of you, and your hormones are high, like in the books. Mine wasn't hormonal, or anything else. Mine was a definite—I've been totally screwed over, and how can I live, how can I look in the mirror? If someone treats me this bad, how can I be worth anything? I've always had a really high self-esteem, too high, and too strong. I have always been the strongest person I've known, strong-willed, nothing could get me down. How could I, of all people, let someone rape me, let someone come in and do these things to me? I wouldn't say it was postpartum depression, I'd say it was postrape depression. I don't think it had anything to do with the baby, except that I felt sorry for him. I still do, that he had to go through that. He has trouble waking up, he is the worst waker-upper I've ever seen in my life. I really think that he was woken up three weeks before he would even have thought about it, and in a really rotten way. He was lost, he is such a good boy, so sweet, I still feel just terrible when I think of it. That was one thing that depressed me when I came home. Oh, this poor baby, look what he's been through. But I wouldn't say it was the blues.

Vicky might have felt the losses described in childbirth books about feeling empty now that the baby was born, and feeling overwhelmed about her new motherhood role. Instead, the trauma was her entire focus. She pointed out to me sections in several books about postpartum depression that had contributed to her feeling crazy after the birth, because none of them mentioned what she was going through, particularly her rage about what occurred. This contributed to her belief that she was the only one "in the world" that this had happened to, the only one that hated how her baby was born.

Despair

Vicky's birth experience is one example of how despair can emerge afterwards. If there is also an undercurrent of despair in a woman's life that is not fully recognized, the postbirth period could trigger its release. This new tiny being is completely vulnerable. If the mother herself has doubts and fears undermining her own belief in the worthwhile nature of life, that baby, dependent on her to sustain its own life, will challenge her despair. This potential exists no matter how the baby was born, and this psychic battle can be her most difficult. If she can win, then she has traversed her own valley shadowed with death.

She feels in danger of falling down a bottomless, dark pit, and she might or might not be able to throw her baby to the side before she slides down. Few chapters on this pit are found in her pregnancy and childbirth books. There are no tools outlined for how to fill it with life and light, or how to tie the baby to safety as she feels herself sliding.

The black pit of despair came to me in many forms: self-doubt about what I had done to cause the prolapsed cord, my lack of awareness of the threat to my baby's well-being, and thoughts about how my body was ripped open. Those first months of Evan's life were torn between wanting to be with him, not feeling as though I deserved to be with him, and doubting my ability to be a good mother. His survival was all that kept me alive those first few months.

Especially when the baby's birth feels like a rape, or the terror seems to eat through a woman, new seeds of despair are sown, and any seed previously present may have grown. The adjustment to her baby is like a finish line she cannot reach, no matter how fast she runs. She feels dead inside, and the future is truly unknown. She needs to take back her life, but she may not know that is possible.

If this state exists, then it must be lived through, and it always takes longer than the time frame expected. A woman may physically ache from emotional pain. Pain is always in front of her and behind her, and a woman walks with it always. In this kind of situation, a new mother may find herself discussing postpartum depression, but she

needs to talk about trauma and how to cope with an unacceptable loss
or an experience that was unbelievable until now.

She has unwillingly tapped a deep part of herself, and though she
may not want to look at it or reverse the direction of anger from inward
to outward, that is where she needs to go next.

A woman becomes pregnant and she often gets more than she
bargained for: a pregnancy, birth, and possibly trauma. With the experiences of this new baby, the powerful potential for change and discovery of her deep places is also present. Though not originally desired,
opportunity emerges in this difficult time for strong, effective, cut-to-
the-quick healing. Giving birth has the potential of ten years of therapy to open a woman up, given the chance. Just as a seed of despair
grows and opens up the bottomless black pit, a seed of hope or sense of
belonging in the world also grows to become a solid core within oneself.

MOTHER'S WORK

Birth and the baby act as catalysts for deep and lasting change in
a mother's life. All areas of life are impacted and require adjustment.
For many women, there is a need to focus on creating a new balance
between work outside of the home and inside of the home.

I cannot write about or discuss postpartum adjustment without
including work issues. Much of the difficulty after my first son's birth
was in reconciling feelings of attachment with the need to make money
and eventually to maintain my career. Recovering from trauma during
this first year as a new mother was integrally tied in to this conflict.

Each woman has different needs for time with children and time
away and a different pattern in which she can best nurture her family. Flexibility is essential to create the best possible situation. The
spectrum is very wide from one end, working outside the home full
time, to the other end, working at home full time with children. The
goal to work outside or inside the home cannot be dictated to a woman.
If she tries to put aside her sense of frustration, pain of separation, or
fear of losing herself in the black pit, then depression may readily
ensue. This balance needs to be taken seriously.

Bias and conflict occur no matter what choice is made; knowing
this will help a woman cope. The stereotypes of either a homemaker or
a career woman who leaves her lonely children do no one justice. The
choice of working part-time may alleviate some pressures, but others
occur as several worlds are juggled each day or week.

My personal journey on the work-children vista has included all
of the above. I had to sample each lifestyle before I could accept my

own variation; I had many negative messages about each role that
needed to be addressed. Eventually all roles came together to complete
the picture, but it has been a difficult task.

With my first son's arrival, I was immediately challenged to cut
down from full-time. After doing so, I was then faced with the financial
consequences. I struggled with others' perceived or imagined expectations of being a mother. I also had to face my own fear of turning into
a negative mother image, a woman who has no brain and only wears
slippers.

> We were deeply in debt from the cesarean, my extra time off,
> and not returning immediately full-time. Severe financial conse-
> quences faced us if I did not work. My head recited this statement
> with cold logic. My heart cried, "I cannot leave this barely born baby
> with whom I am having a love affair beyond my dreams! No, thank
> you very much. I can still feel the earth's heartbeat through my feet
> reminding me of my purpose—to nurture this child and nurture
> myself."
>
> Those first afternoons away from him made it clear how and
> why others managed with no salary for six months or longer in order
> to be with their children. If we had had any resources to draw from,
> I would have done so. Welfare was even considered.
>
> But stronger than financial worries was the maternal instinct
> which drove me to make sure Evan was okay. His cry pierced my
> heart and I rushed to hold him each time. When I got home at night
> we would be on the couch, Evan laying on my stomach, and I could
> still imagine him inside of me, as his little sleeping body blocked the
> view of my feet. I felt his heart beat on my chest as he felt mine, as
> it was so little time ago when he was within me instead of outside.
>
> All of a sudden I wanted to be a homemaker. That breed of
> woman who talks baby talk, stays home, is involved in her children's
> lives, who is able to fold laundry and calm a crying child while trying
> to watch the news. Previously this lifestyle had threatened me. I
> didn't want a mind filled only with children, didn't want to look like a
> mother—wearing old, messy clothes, always in a rush, looking
> worn-out. I didn't want to go to family restaurants and leave in a
> hurry when a toddler had a tantrum. I didn't want a twenty-four-hour
> job, taking naps when the children did to catch up on sleep.
>
> I had worked hard to be successful, spent ten years in col-
> lege, earned a Ph.D., and had a thriving private practice. I didn't
> want to be dependent on a man or be afraid that if on my own I
> couldn't support myself. I had job security and was capable of sup-
> porting myself, even an entire family. But with a baby everything

was different. Suddenly I did not *want* to be the breadwinner; my mom job was taking a lot more effort and was a lot more pleasurable than I thought it would be.

Five years before Evan was born I wrote my master's thesis on dual-income families. Even from an academic viewpoint, the situation was beyond difficult. The only couples not completely besieged by stress were those who made enough money to hire a nanny or housekeeper—basically a "wife". Everyone else scrambled trying to make ends meet, to find adequate day care, to meet the dual demands of job and home. My study was about dual-employed blue-collar couples instead of highly educated professional couples, who are most often the subjects of study. The research provided one surprising conclusion: marital satisfaction increased with the number of children. This result interested me; with more children, the stress of working and finances must increase—yet those couples were happier. My thesis, academic in nature and requiring empirical evidence and discussion, buried this finding in the discussion at the end.

Now, after his birth, I understood that finding. And to my surprise, a traditional lifestyle which would allow me to stay home with Evan had intense appeal; five years ago that thought was unimaginable.

But I didn't want that lifestyle, either. I seesawed between total career and total housewife; I needed both. Why did it have to be all or nothing? We would sit down with the immediate debt, over 6,000 dollars owed to credit cards and the hospital, and I would panic. Yet leaving Evan to go work was so painful.

Though I wanted more than anything to be with Evan, my life was built on the premise that I would work and be a success. Work was the most life-giving thing I had discovered until Evan. The thought of cutting down to part-time felt essential, but it meant betraying my whole former life. To have had the whole first year just to be with Evan would have been humane, but I couldn't give that opportunity to myself even if it were possible.

If I had to work in the outside world, there was nothing I liked better than my job as a psychologist. I still enjoyed working with clients, being a part of other people's healing. But every minute of paperwork or phone calls or learning about new legislation was resented. A balance was created by ignoring whatever I didn't have to know, by doing only what was necessary. I began to skip meetings, and turned a blind ear to gossip about insurance companies, preferring to not worry about whether mental health coverage continued and for how long.

Time spent with my son was sacred. I lost clients because of reduced hours, some were angry with me for not being as available. And I was happy to treasure those hours and keep the relationship with Evan as top priority.

The desire to be with my son, infinitely stronger than expected and sprung from nowhere, unleashed what I call the Dumb Woman.

Being the Mom of a small child, to be a caregiver and immerse myself in laundry, toys, parks and cooking, was a meditation with bursts of joy. Sitting on the kitchen floor with Evan while he ate his snack of corn puffs did not involve a concrete mind, it involved all of me enjoying him. He would put one at a time in his mouth, chasing one that rolled under the refrigerator, saying, "Oopies" for oopsie.

When I felt lost, standing there in the middle of the kitchen floor, wondering what to do first as my eye caught eight things at once, not wanting to do any of them, I would first load one plate into the dishwasher. Then another, finding the jars to be recycled and the lids to be thrown out as I went along, cleaning enough of the counter to wipe it off. By then the task had become satisfying instead of overwhelming. With this clean countertop there was now room to cook dinner—the sink was clean, so that washing a head of lettuce was a straightforward task unhampered by dirty dishes. There was even room to open a cookbook. Then I would move on to another area of the house, or was satisfied. Then Evan's cry for attention was just fine. We would sit on the couch with his blanket and do nothing.

But I had this image of a housewife, and even dreamed of her as the other woman. I dreamed that *Michael is going off to have a baby with this other woman, the Dumb Woman, he is choosing her over me. Even though we already have a child and are married, he is going to travel with her, and they are going to make a baby together. I'm willing to stay with him even though he feels this way, but he doesn't care. I confront him and he agrees that I've lost him. I am so angry, I yell, "You are going to leave me, and I'm going to have to be the single parent, I'm going to have to start all over, find a place for Evan and I to live while I get a new job, and you're just going to up and leave?" He is calmly, passively walking around as I yell, and I push him onto the bed, wanting a response from him. After knocking him out briefly, he comes to and says, "You'd better knock it off, Lynn, you're starting to get dangerous."*

This Dumb Woman had little intelligence, could only talk about how to make popsicles. Her hair didn't look good—*could* not look good when you're a Dumb Woman. The lowest of low work was what this woman did, she mended clothing for a living. She wore dumpy clothes, and felt dumpy. Could it get any worse, my vision of motherhood? Yes.

"You don't deserve to have it so easy," a voice said. "This isn't real work. One kid is nothing, heck, a real woman would have at least three. Then at least you could justify staying home. Besides, you've got all that education, and now look, I was right all along about you. You're going to stay home and be a mother."

I couldn't hate this woman more, this woman in me that was so demeaned. I needed to love the Dumb Woman, just as in my dream Michael loved her—enough to leave me. *Leave behind all that old, no-longer-needed baggage.*

"Here", a guardian angel says, "let me take those bags for you." They are taken out of my hands, I have no choice, and watch them being spirited away, feeling uncomfortable, left with only the clothes on my back. But those old suitcases full of used-up, not-cared-about items are hardly missed. I do not worry, knowing I have the resources to get what is needed as I walk into the future.

In the real world, working less and being home more meant making less money, and more financial dependence on Michael. I would be giving up my professional status, and was afraid of fading into the woodwork. I could imagine old friends and colleagues saying, "Whatever happened to Lynn Madsen?"

"Oh, she decided to stay home with her child, I haven't seen her for years."

Like I died, or would lose my mind, because the Dumb Woman doesn't ever use her mind. I as the Dumb Woman would greet Michael when he came home in the evenings and hang on his coat, begging for news of the outside world. He would brush me off, disdainful of my low work. I was so afraid of what he would think of me. Afraid of what everyone would think of me. I would grovel at my husband's feet, a slave.

No, when Michael walked through the door he might be tired, but he always had a hug for me, and would scoop Evan up and sit on the couch saying, "How was your day? Isn't this kid the greatest? I have a great life."

When Michael was asked what he would think if I stayed home full-time with Evan, he said, "Actually, little of my esteem for you is based on your work. Not that it isn't great what you do. But I love your qualities that are always present." When asked what qualities he meant, he went on, "Your intelligence, your beauty, your creativity, your strength, your resourcefulness."

My jaw dropped. Such a novel thought. I was like a person
facing retirement, scared about an empty life, having no self-worth
unless it was tied to my job. A good feeling stirred deep inside, as
those affirming adjectives sunk in.

The Dumb Woman became my friend. She was smart enough
to put her feet up when she got the chance, instead of taking on a
new project. She could care less what others thought of her—she
knew she was worthy of life. I consulted her; what would the Dumb
Woman do in this case, when Evan was sick? Try to sneak him in
to day care?

"No," said the Dumb Woman, "follow your heart, keep him
home with you, love him up." She was dumb as in dumbsmart. I
began to think she was brilliant. She was the one that pointed out to
me I was moaning for my past life of being child free. Those were
the days, I said. Life was so easy, wasn't it? Untethered—what a
word. Was I tethered by children? What a burden. There was that
old message, a child burdens you for life, takes away your freedom,
your rights to personhood. Part of the old baggage left behind, but
ghosts wafted back in occasionally. The Dumb Woman knows to
open her heart and welcome these children.

Amazing there is a source of love inside of me that can
expand, fill me up. And it has nothing to do with anyone else. It was
there when I was two years old, feeling terrified and hurt. It was
there every single day, and has nourished me in spite of my belief
that I was empty, and wishing someone else would do this work.
This is between me alone, and the universe. The source of love is
located deep within, and pulses with life, it is light-filled, a light
source.

*I jump over the edge of the 5,000-foot cliff to become a home-
maker! Wings sprout out of my shoulders as I soar on my downward descent and journey to a new plateau. I fly, checking out the
terrain, deciding—deciding—where to land, where to plant my garden, build my house, plant my roots all over again. I choose the
perfect place, to become the housewife. Relaxed, harried, happy,
sad, frustrated, content housewife. I choose my place, and bring my
baby bird safely to the new nest. He has travelled well, all snug,
warm, and well fed. He is drowsy, and takes his time to become
alert and check out the new surroundings. Oh, Mom! Where have
you brought us? Will you stay here with us? That would be nice,
Mom. Hey, look! A nice muddy pool in the back yard. Let's go play!*

I worked a bit more, and still spent Fridays with Evan.
Everything became more enjoyably intense. My need for time alone
was tended to carefully. I assuaged my guilt about those hours by

recalling the consequences of anger and resentment if I didn't. I wrote an affirmation for myself.

I can say anything about what is inside me to Michael, and be heard and respected. I share what is happening about money and babies and life dreams and feel entirely safe and valued. I know I am appreciated and what I offer is lovingly accepted. My energy blends harmoniously with my family, and I am blessed at all times. I have a completely balanced lifestyle, working to a satisfaction level. Whenever desired I rest and meditate. I am a homemaker—an expression of spirit. I move at a serene pace, appreciating all the gifts that I have. I clear out no-longer-useful physical or emotional items whenever needed. I accept with love the spirits of my family and environment and community.

The affirmation worked. My envisioned life became possible.

When my own biases and self-hate came to the surface, I could accept this softer, humane side. If I'd had more confidence and less investment in what other people thought of me, it would have been easier to honor my desire to stay home.

After my second son's birth, when Evan was three years old, I took ten months off from work and was a full-time mother for the very first time. I thought this step would resolve the conflict, which still existed. To temporarily let go of my career was one of the greatest acts of faith I ever displayed. Also, because this second birth went wonderfully, I did not have the personal needs of recovery that existed with the first birth. My home time was focused on the new baby and learning how to cope with two children.

This complete commitment to being home and not at the office allowed me to discover things that would have remained hidden. By the time my second baby was four months old, I knew that I *needed* to return to the office, for everyone's sake. I am a good mother, given the opportunity to work outside of the home. This discovery was made only because I had given myself permission to stay home full-time.

I also discovered the joy of losing myself in child-time, a sort of meditation I can now do while picking up toys, playing repetitious games, or simply sitting on the floor with a nonverbal being. I became involved in my neighborhood community, and that will stay with me always.

In some ways being home is more of a challenge, because the myth exists that there is time to relax and have fun. The image of watching television and eating bonbons must have emerged in the fifties and been incredibly powerful, because it's still here, and I've never seen anyone actually do it. Some women do love being home, and cope excellently with the demands of full-time parenting. Vicky's resourcefulness led her to quit her teaching job and open a home day care. She has been happy for several years, home with her own children and others'.

> I quit my job—that's one thing I'm glad about, because I think I would have gone back to work if it hadn't been for how he was born. But he had an esophageal problem because he was born three weeks early, and you couldn't lay him down because he would choke. I didn't feel comfortable with anyone else taking care of him. My aunt was going to baby-sit for him, but she has ten other kids to take care of at her day care, and I didn't feel comfortable that anybody could watch him as well as I could. Now I never leave him anywhere except with my mom, because now I'm the one who has the problem, I can't leave him. I think I became so attached to him because I couldn't hardly move for the first six weeks. It wasn't because I was depressed, it was because I was so infected, so sore, that there was no moving to be done. Really. And so I quit my job, and I would have continued working if I hadn't been so physically wiped out. That's one thing I don't regret. It's worked out well—I needed to be making money, and so a home day care was the best solution. I'm with him all the time, I'm making money, and I do what I think is important.

Vicky's industriousness and passion were relatively easily channelled into her home day care. She fulfills her roles as mother and provider, and is content at this time.

Each solution must be extremely tailor-made. Vicky's situation is right for her, mine is right for me. The goal of balance and satisfaction is not always immediately forthcoming. Experimentation may be necessary. I paid for my search with a truly fluctuating income. This required flexibility from my family; for me, the price was worth it. Now I strike a balance that keeps me whole; it keeps me connected with my children and home. My nightmares of destroying various parts of my life have stopped. Others find different ways to resolve their own relationships between home, office, and wherever and whomever else. What needs to be confirmed is the search, and alternative solutions need to be respected. When the home-work dilemma goes unacknowledged or is minimized, a woman runs the risk of depression or becoming out of balance. Then she has little to give anyone: herself, her family, or the work environment.

When there is a need for many options but only one option exists, either to stay home or to maintain an already existing job, a new mother needs and deserves support and understanding for the difficulties involved. Instead, minimization is frequently offered: "Oh, you'll adjust. Women have been taking care of babies for thousands of years," or "My mother was a single parent with five young kids who worked to support us, and she pulled it off." Postpartum adjustment is no small task. It deserves care and attention, and is a lot of work. This work is undertaken to allow the room to love and enjoy our babies to the best of our capabilities.

As a new mother discovers ways to cope with the incredible adventure of a baby in her life, she understands the stress attributable to balancing this new role with others, and what stress is due to the wounds of birth. She understands that both need attention.

FOR WORK ON YOUR OWN

Question One: What have you thought was the meaning of postpartum depression? What is your personal definition of postpartum depression? As a new mother, have you been depressed or in despair? Have you acknowledged this with anyone else? What have you attributed these feelings to?

Question Two: Where are you on the spectrum?
Work at home full time with children ———Work outside the home full time

Have you been other places on the spectrum? Where are you most comfortable, and why?

FOR FURTHER READING

Cowan, Carolyn, and Cowan, Philip. (1992) *When Partners Become Parents.* New York: Basic Books.
Crosby, Faye. (1991) *Juggling: The Unexpected Advantages of Balancing Career and Home for Women and Their Families.* New York: Free Press.
Dalton, Katharina. (1989) *Depression after Childbirth: How to Recognize and Treat Postnatal Illness.* Oxford, UK: Oxford University Press.
Goldman, Katherine. (1993) *My Mother Worked and I Turned Out Okay.* New York: Villard.
Jack, Dana Crowley. (1991) *Silencing the Self: Women and Depression.* Cambridge, MA: Harvard University Press.
Sanders, Darcie, and Bullen, Martha. (1992) *Staying Home: From Full-Time Professional to Full-Time Parent.* Boston: Little, Brown.

Sanford, Linda, and Donovan, Mary Ellen. (1984) *Women and Self-Esteem.* New York: Penguin.

Sears, William. (1985) *The Fussy Baby: How to Bring Out the Best in Your High-Need Child.* Minneapolis, MN: La Leche.

PART II

PICKING UP THE PIECES, ACCEPTING THE GIFTS OF BIRTH, AND MOVING FORWARD

The birth of a child may involve pain, trauma, and other negative, powerful components. But those forces also hold life and the opportunity for healing, given the chance.

When my second baby was due in three days, I whined to my old friend Catherine, who was our labor coach for the first birth, "I'm afraid it's all going to happen again, he's gonna be born just like Evan—I won't dilate, he'll be face up and the cord will prolapse, and I'll be cut open again. And I don't want to be two weeks late again. I hate being pregnant, I'll be pregnant forever, it sucks." I went on and on. Catherine eventually said, "You have an opportunity to heal, Lynn. None of those things have to happen. And even if they do, you have an opportunity to heal."

I grumbled, as there was distinct displeasure in looking at this apparent misfortune and fear as an opportunity, especially to heal. I still felt wounded and was afraid of more damage. Yet another door wrenched open a crack, as I saw pain and fear in a different light. Several days later (one day past my due date), I went into labor. Throughout, I kept up a running commentary while experiencing back labor and other challenges: "This is an opportunity to heal." And though my voice was wry and slightly sarcastic, there was also humor and the potential for good things to happen. Who knows how much difference this one attitude made? Perhaps the outcome would have been exactly the same. Yet the phrase has stuck with me.

I do not wish this opportunity to learn from trauma or pain for anyone, yet here is the paradox: if such things do happen, then I hope there are gifts from having learned the hard way. These gifts are powerful, and they will continue to keep on giving throughout one's life.

A woman calls out, speaks out, and moves forward. The trauma is defined, the power of denial diminished. Seemingly all she accomplishes is to know how difficult her challenges are. There are more layers in which to dive and explore; each time she uncovers a layer, she will become more whole and more coherent. A woman who has the courage to seek healing has the courage to become healthy.

Part II includes forays into strong emotions, action steps a woman will take such as deciding whether to become pregnant again, valuing each step taken, telling her story and listening to those of others, and discovering what acceptance and forgiveness means.

AFFIRM ALL ATTEMPTS AT SELF-EMPOWERMENT

6

No matter what action a woman takes toward healing, gaining strength, and making choices to improve her situation, each and every action needs to be affirmed. Any movement toward healing, no matter what its outcome, will make a difference. Movement towards health is movement away from the sinkhole of depression, denial, and self-hate.

A friend once said, "You're either moving toward or away from something all the time. There's no such thing as being stuck." Being stuck is an illusion, for nonaction has as many consequences as action. Imagine a woman stepping toward healing and strength. With each step, she learns and grows, so that her steps become more confident and fruitful. Not taking any steps means loss of the entire healing path. But she can begin at any time; there is no wrong time to begin a healing journey. Timing is different for everyone; an individual knows her own internal clock. She knows when to take action, when to recognize feelings, and when to address her own power.

For example, if anger is discovered and embraced, fuel now exists with which to take more steps. This can occur at any time, from immediately after giving birth to ten or more years later. Anger will help her move, propel her to the next step. Ideas spring forth of what she wants to do, and now is the time to pick up the phone, pen, or shovel.

Ellen knew right away that something was wrong with her birth experience. One of the first steps she took was attempting to talk with her doctor at her six-week checkup.

> I felt angry about the birth, and wanted to get apologies from my obstetrician. I wanted to say to her, look, what went wrong here, why did things work out the way they did? I wanted to know if there was some medical reason for everything that happened, and

whether I should be prepared for it all to happen again. I didn't get any satisfaction from her, I wasn't very assertive about it, I don't like confrontations. All I could tell her was about being upset about the vacuum extraction. I didn't realize that I was upset about all the other interventions yet. You know, a lot of people have had bigger babies yet. I guess I just felt betrayed.

I did do a lot of thinking about it. I let go of the anger to a large degree after that six-week visit, because I didn't feel it would do me any good to just keep feeling angry about it. I was not going to go back to her, and I never saw her again after that, but there was a lot of rehashing inside me.

Ellen could have been more articulate and assertive with her doctor. But she opened her mouth and good words came out. The doctor did not provide a satisfactory explanation, but the answer Ellen did receive made her think. Obviously, not returning to her obstetrician was a clear message about her dissatisfaction. Later, she realized that the "big-baby explanation" was not enough, and she sought further information. This conversation was a more than adequate nudge for Ellen to move toward rather than away from healing. She continued to seek information.

Then I did start to do some reading, I don't remember what it was specifically, because I was still reading *American Baby Magazine*, which didn't provide much help on anything. I did find *Mothering* real soon after he was born, and maybe it was something in there that enlightened me and got my consciousness upraised. I started thinking, things probably didn't have to be the way that they were.

I got a book by a midwife out of the library. It was about the Amish [*A Wise Birth*], and it was real inspiring, because she was talking about natural childbirths, and a whole different spectrum of people. It included women who were really young to mothers who were forty or fifty. The babies were all born at home, there's no transport to the hospital, and I thought, wow, what is it these people have that I don't have? That got me to realize there was another way to do these things. She talked about why she became a midwife, and lights came on in my head, and I thought, Wow! she saw the same things in the medical system that bothered me. I started to realize that I had walked into it, though I had hoped I had a choice. Now I thought that I could have a home birth. But if something went wrong, I'm such a perfectionist, I would blame myself because I hadn't done everything I could do to insure safety. I'm starting to come around to the idea that life is risky, birth is risky, things don't always work out.

Affirm any attempt, any step, rather than belittle oneself for not having done enough. More can always be accomplished. To believe that the efforts being made are inadequate is a backslide into a shame pit. A woman again pulls herself forward by affirming she is learning and making progress. Affirm each action as an accomplishment in and of itself.

Ellen began to see how many more choices she had about birth-related events. Instead of berating herself for past choices, she persisted in her search for answers to what happened during Jason's birth, and empowered herself with new information for the future. Ellen became pregnant again, and was further challenged by what appeared to be a worse birthing situation than her first birth.

> With my second pregnancy, I realized how close I had come during Jason's birth to having a cesarean. I knew that I needed to do something different, and I knew that I could find a more satisfying atmosphere. So I called a number of people at ICAN [International Cesarean Awareness Network] who helped me find a clinic that would meet my criteria. This clinic had a group of midwives with a woman o.b., and they handed me their philosophy about not intervening, and I thought, Oh! This is great! It was really good for me to realize there was a place like that. I began to realize that I'm stronger than I think, and the importance of my attitude. I had to feel empowered and that I could do it. Not feel like it was the doctor's job to deliver my baby. I began to realize it's my job to push the baby out, and I could do it without any help. The help is there to support me, but not to do it for me.

> I got going with this clinic for prenatals, and everything went along smoothly until I had a bleed at six months. The ultrasound they did made me realize that I wasn't going to have a natural childbirth because of the placenta previa.

> I kept having bleeds, and before the birth I was in the hospital for two weeks. I had a real bad bleed, and I was contracting, which made me bleed more. So they put me first on magnesium sulfate, and later on Tributalene. I felt sorry for myself being in the hospital, but I felt really sorry for Jason, who was eighteen months old. His mother disappeared in the middle of the night, and I had different people taking care of him. And then of course I was going to have a premature baby, and was afraid they would have to take him right away with a cesarean. I was afraid he wouldn't be ready, and I would have to deal with those problems. But those two weeks in the hospital ended up making a big difference for him, he didn't have to

be on the intensive care unit.

I had four or five ultrasounds; some were to see how the baby was doing, and he was in great shape. The other ones were to see if the placenta had moved, and it did move a little bit. The morning of the surgery, my doctor came in and she said, "I've been looking at this ultrasound and only the very edge of the placenta is covering the cervix. If you really want a vaginal delivery, I could support you in it, because there is a chance that the pressure of the baby's head would tamp off the edge of the placenta." But what that meant was that I would have to go off the drugs, and if I didn't go into labor right away, I would go home and wait for it to happen. Or I could start bleeding again, no one knew what would happen. If I started bleeding again I would be even more anemic, and I might end up with an emergency cesarean anyway, if this tamping off thing didn't work. The doctor made me make the decision. I said, "What would you advise?" She said, "It depends on how much of a risk taker you are." I said, "Well, I'm not much of a risk taker." The doctor said she could definitely support me either way. That's when I decided to not risk more bleeding and possibly an emergency cesarean. I decided to go on with the scheduled cesarean. It looked to me like my odds of having a cesarean were pretty great anyway, so why not have one under controlled circumstances.

Most doctors wouldn't have given me that choice. I felt better afterwards, too. I was so wiped out after Jason's birth, the trauma, the surprises, being so anemic. I was still anemic after Henry's birth, but I was able to go to Target a week later. He was born on a Thursday, I went home on Monday, and that Friday my mom, Grandma, and I went to Target. I was so desperate to get out of the house, I had been on bed rest for three months. I wasn't sorry. I didn't overdo it, I just felt that much better even after a cesarean. And it's the attitude. Yeah, I've got this incision, and it hurts, but mentally I didn't feel victimized. Except I was separated from Henry right after the birth.

That was the only bad part. I was so calm because the cesarean wasn't a surprise. If you can go into it with your eyes open it helps. Knowing that you're going to have a cesarean, being able to talk to the people, and actually seeing the operating room. They answered all the questions I wanted answered, so I felt good about being in control. By having it scheduled, there was no emergency, no rush to get it done. They shaved my hair, put in the catheter. I had a morphine spinal, and that was wonderful. It was very effective, and there wasn't anything sticking out of my back like during my first labor with Jason. The anesthesiologist explained and I read about the tugging sensation. I felt prepared. The bad part was they took Henry immediately away, and I didn't get to see him. I had been on magnesium sulfate and Tributalene for two weeks, and their concern was that the magnesium levels in his body would prevent him from metabolizing food. He could start throwing up and he would get dehydrated, and it would start a vicious cycle. I had talked to the house pediatrician before the birth, and he assured me there wouldn't be any reason why the baby and I would be separated. I thought he was the one who would make the final decision. But my doctor called in the neonatologist, and she got a different one than she had worked with in the past. This one was real conservative, and he decided that the baby would be taken to the nursery. I was real upset, I saw him for about a second, and he looked great. He cried right away, and they were just amazed at how big he was, five and a half pounds at four weeks early. I was just pissed, and I felt really helpless, because I was on the gurney. I couldn't go get that baby. Other than that, the birth worked out as well as it possibly could, considering the circumstances. It made all the difference because I made the choices. Looking at it clinically, it was more dramatic, but emotionally, it was better.

Making the choices enhanced my power because I was more involved with the whole process. That's the difference; to have a caregiver who cares, who understands. She did throw me a curve at the last minute, when the cesarean was scheduled for noon, and at ten o'clock she said, "Well, we could do this." But it was my choice. If I had gone the other way, my doctor might not have been there for my delivery. Someone else could have been on call. Part of my decision was knowing my doctor would deliver my baby. But it was my decision. It was traumatic. There are lots of things that happen in your life, but you've got to play the cards you are dealt.

I still don't know if I can have another baby the way I want to. But I figure I learned more things and I have more things to learn. I thought that I could do something to prevent any intervention. The fear was there, and still is. But on the other hand, the fear is less now that I've had the cesarean, and it wasn't such a bad experience. It was easier than all the interventions that happened during my first delivery. It was planned, and it was necessary. There was no question in my mind that I had to have it for my son to be born. Otherwise I was sure I would have bled to death, or he would have died because he couldn't get out.

Ellen did make the best of a difficult situation. She lost the opportunity for a nonintervened labor, but she grew stronger and recovered faster because of all of her efforts, and because her environment nurtured her. There were still elements beyond her control; this birth included an unexpected separation from her new baby that lasted forty-eight hours. Ellen still knew she had done all she could. As soon as she was mobile, she was in the nursery waiting for her first opportunity to breast-feed and hold her new son. She learned how to make good decisions for herself and her babies, and that wisdom will be with her always.

When steps toward reparation don't go as planned, it is tempting to blame our efforts as not being strong enough, smart enough, courageous enough, or just not enough. Step back to see the progress and good work. Give credit for what has been accomplished rather than what has not. Notice the movement and the increase of strength, experience, and knowledge. The pursuit of perfection is truly an imperfect goal, prone toward failure.

Instead, affirm oneself by praising all efforts and accomplishments. Affirm the path of healing, wherever it leads.

FOR WORK ON YOUR OWN

Question One: Have you ever abandoned a goal because of the fear of not completing it? If you give yourself permission to begin the goal and take only the first step, would that make the fear smaller? Then after beginning the goal, make sure there is a reward of some kind. Accept an encouraging word of support from a friend and/or yourself. Create a written log of the experience. Pat yourself on the back. Do a dance in the kitchen. Buy a magazine you've wanted to read.

Question Two: Perhaps a goal's results have turned out differently than planned and you feel disappointment. Do you negate the entire experience? Is there a way to affirm the results, if only to learn that humility can be borne with dignity? Add the experience to a growing bank of knowledge, and trust that there will be other opportunities to succeed and also learn from. Examine this unexpected direction for new destinations or variations of the original goal that can meet your needs in different ways.

FOR FURTHER READING

Armstrong, Penny, and Feldman, Sheryl. (1990). *A Wise Birth*. New York: Morrow.

Kaufman, Gershen, and Raphael, Lev. (1983) *The Dynamics of Power*. Cambridge, MA: Schenkman.

Sanford, Linda, and Donovan, Mary Ellen. (1984) *Women and Self-Esteem*. New York: Penguin.

MAYBE
ANOTHER BABY

7

Some women have only one baby because they do not know that healing from trauma is possible or that birth can be different from what they experienced the first time. Others can hardly wait to become pregnant again, hoping for a different experience from the first birth. Neither of these approaches is a guarantee of avoiding future pain. A subsequent birth will be what it is: perhaps a repeat experience, a healing experience, a heartbreak, or something in between. Who knows? Or the decision may be clearly made not to have another baby, either because of family plans already completed, or because a woman knows what is right for her and does not want to give birth again.

With the decision to have another baby, commitment to taking all the risks along with all the joy is made. One of the advantages to being a seasoned parent is that at least part of the illusion of parenting has been realized, including the sense of control regarding the outcome of a child's birth and life. When the unexpected has already occurred, there's more acceptance of surprises. A subsequent birth plan needs to include acceptance of the possibility of a similar trauma occurring again.

After the birth of my first son, I was very surprised at the strong desire for more babies. Even while still at the hospital, I told Michael I knew I wanted three children. He himself wasn't ready to talk about it. My desire to birth vaginally was intense after coming so close during labor. I had a visceral desire that completely contradicted what had just happened and what I intellectually knew to be wise. The issue of another baby also pushed and pulled our marriage.

In spite of a difficult birth, the power of creating a baby was intoxicating. The instant love and connection to his body, so soft and small, and his spirit, so bright, was a greater joy than anything previously known. I knew then why people had more than one child, because a child was wonderful.

I wanted another chance to give birth, to do it right. To actually get pregnant would have been insane, not being healed from the first birth—emotionally, physically, or spiritually. Yet going through pregnancy in any form, eternal morning sickness, whatever it took, would be worth the experience of the internal rhythm of vaginally delivering, of pushing a baby out into the world. I hated that my baby had to enter the world through my stomach.

But I hated more that he almost died, he was oxygen-starved, in a dried up womb with a worn-out placenta, I hated more that he was suffering. I wished to get rid of this desire to give birth again, wanted to be able to gladly, freely have done whatever it took to have a healthy baby, throw me on the table, get him out of me, please, as fast as you can, oh God, I hope he's all right, please let him be all right, I'm breathing deeply for you, baby, hang in there, you'll be out soon, into loving arms.

Maybe a bargain could be struck with God. I was not convinced that I did not do something to deserve what happened. "Okay, God. I will go through another cesarean, and will accept my fate if you will give me another healthy child. I ask for your mercy for a safe birth."

My fantasy desire to be pregnant again was separate from our sex life. We were definitely using birth control again. I laughed, thinking of a conversation with my friend during the time when we were trying to conceive, when I was so high on having unprotected sex. Yes, there came a time when I was very glad for birth control.

We kept Evan home with one or the other of us until he was five months old, possible to do since we both worked part-time with flexible hours. I only worked what was necessary to keep my practice going and pay the minimum bills. Full-time work was no longer an option; leaving him part-time was painful enough. Each week we had a budget meeting to figure out how to meet expenses, and to coordinate our work schedules.

Michael sat at the dining room table, writing down the amounts of each debt—hospital, credit card advances, monthly expenses. "If we can come up with seven hundred dollars more, we can meet the minimum payments for this month."

"I can't deposit more money until next week. We could call the hospital, offer them a payment plan." There was a lead ball of anger in my stomach, my words were spoken in a low monotone.

"That's not a bad idea. There's just no place else to get the money," Michael responded.

"Maybe we could cut back on groceries," I suggested.

"That's ridiculous. We're doing fine, there'll be more money."

"No there won't, we need to cut our expenses more." I wanted him to suffer, stop drinking Diet Coke as penance, as though that would make him see things my way.

I wondered just exactly what I was doing with this man, and at the same time wanted another baby so badly, I thought of staying with him just to have access to sperm. Blind rage. A second baby was going to have to wait.

Imagining another cesarean was terrifying. Now, after experiencing one, I knew that they existed and happened. I went back and read those chapters previously skipped about cesareans and infant loss. I read *Silent Knife* and was grateful for the chapter where an M.D. graphically described the actual operation, and how my entire uterus was removed to the outside of my body to be stitched up. I began to know that I could live through a cesarean if it happened again, and could tolerate one more scalpel cut, even with some degree of serenity, because I wanted another child.

It took many months to sort through our issues as a couple, and to decide how much of my desire was to "make up" for what happened with the first birth. Once I became clear that yes, I definitely wanted another child, regardless of how he or she would arrive, and once Michael and I renegotiated our marriage to solidly include this commitment to an expanding family, we attempted to conceive. After we did conceive another child, I knew I still had work to do about the first birth in order to feel safe and confident.

THE INFLUENCE OF PAST BIRTHS WHEN PREGNANT

Any reminder of the reproductive cycle may activate unpleasant memories and associations. Part of healing is to reclaim the entire cycle, from having sex again after birth, having a complete menstrual cycle, to another conception and birth. For a woman who is done with childbearing, her job is to love her body again, love its power to create, whether it's a baby or the ability to get through the day. For me, every step of the reproductive cycle needed to be reclaimed.

Having sex again represented the whole cycle that could begin again: creativity, conception, pregnancy, baby. This potential was particularly felt after giving birth so recently. I was scared of it and attracted to it at the same time. Each period's arrival reflected my ambivalence. The potential to create was within me, but I was relieved not to be pregnant. I did not trust my body to conceive, and was afraid of failing.

Many months later, after reclaiming my body, we began trying for our second baby. With each stage of reproduction, memories came to me. Attempting conception the second time was no easier than the first, and brought back the same highs and lows, hopes and fears. After a year of efforts, we did conceive, then miscarried after three months. After the third conception, I gradually settled into this new, yet familiar, pregnancy. I hoped it would all be different, easier because I knew some of what was ahead. Instead, this pregnancy encompassed all of my birth history, including hopes and dreams, grief, the same morning sickness, and a whole new life.

As a woman journeys on the path of her second and other pregnancies and births, she benefits by using each memory. Each association can be used to recall a past birth or pregnancy. Give it its due. Grieve as needed. Know one's fears whenever possible. Be amazed at the similarities and intensity of recalled feelings that one fervently had hoped were gone for good. Affirm this new pregnancy at the same time; there is room for both memories and the present. This is especially true when there has been the death of an infant. If loss of a baby was also experienced, then acknowledge the fear of another loss, another death—it will be a companion through a subsequent pregnancy. Appropriately, a mother will be reminded of the baby who died no matter what, particularly as another baby grows and is born. Expand awareness to include anticipation of the future as well as memories of the past.

Previous births are part of a woman's history, and will influence an upcoming birth more than she expects. As discussed in chapter 4, recognition of unresolved, buried, or traumatic issues is a valuable tool with which to go into labor. Then at least one knows which dragons are being fought, and the barriers that block an effective labor can more easily be broken down.

Pregnancy is a good time for sorting, healing, and building strength with whatever building blocks remain from a previous birth. Associations from the past pregnancy, labor, and delivery emerge, and if a woman acknowledges them to herself with someone she trusts, she has a better chance at changing her history. Telling her birth story, recognizing her fears, carefully choosing her caregivers, rehearsing labor and delivery—all provide a foundation for a good, safe birth. The more conscientiously these tasks are done, the more tools and confidence she will bring with her as labor begins.

For example, during my VBAC (vaginal birth after cesarean), I made conscious efforts both to make the experience different and to acknowledge the similarities to the first birth. In early labor, I knew, as an experienced mother does, that it could go on for quite a while. A friend agreed to take me to the YMCA for a swim. I spent an enjoyable hour in the deep end, living out my fantasy of laboring immersed in water while floating, gently treading water, and swimming.

I was aware of my fear during early labor, when I was about two centimeters dilated, that history could repeat itself. I told Julie, my labor coach, all I knew about this fear, and then the labor continued. When I was six centimeters dilated, I again remembered the first birth; this was when the prolapsed cord had been discovered and steps toward a cesarean had been taken. If I had not rehashed and accepted the first birth, I would have been more likely to repeat the pattern of distress due to my fear. I may have ended up with a cesarean done either at my request or due to my body's failure to progress. During the second birth, after the six-centimeter point I was a first-time mother, never having experienced transition or pushing out a baby. I was amazed, like any first-time mother, at the whole experience.

Some aspects of labor were the same. With each similarity to the first birth, I worked hard to breathe in a sense of safety and power. I had back labor, requiring the palms of someone's hands pushing with all their might on my lower back with each contraction. I threw up upon arrival at the hospital. These details mimicked the first birth, and by knowing my fear each time I was reminded, I was able to stay focused and calm. I could reassure myself that I was doing extremely well, and was also able to perceive how this labor was different from the first one.

When my ketones were checked they were high enough that the nurse and midwife wanted to start an IV. I said, "No! Find another way." I was adamant about no needles or tubes coming out of or going into me. Before the birth I had arranged waivers for both an IV and continuous monitoring, which are both standard procedures for VBAC births at the hospital. My midwife Clara said if I could keep drinking juices, she'd monitor the ketones and let me be for now. Because of my intense reactions toward these reminders of the first birth, I was highly motivated to find other ways of coping. I drank that juice without gagging by pure will power. Here are details of the birth.

I labor in the bathtub in subdued light, Michael and Julie and Clara sitting beside the tub, my companions in creating a peaceful, trusting birth. As my neck stiffens or my rump becomes cold, I change sides. At the beginning of each contraction I say to Julie, "Now." And she softly says the affirmation we have negotiated, "Welcome it. Let it be strong, let the energy flow through you, let it do its work. You are safe. The baby is safe. Your body knows exactly what to do. Feel that cervix open up, like a flower blossoming, feel the baby move down, pressing on the cervix, helping it open, on the cervix that is so soft, it just gives way to the pressure of the baby's head." I need her words, though I know the content by heart.

After a few hours, Clara asks me to get out to be checked. Wrapped in a big towel I totter to the toilet and actually pee. "I peed!" I exclaim, and no one understands this significance. It is a major triumph, proof that this labor is different from the first. Clara looks at the ketone stick; they are still high, and she ups the calorie content by feeding me spoonfuls of honey, which works. I have dilated to seven centimeters, also evidence that my body is functioning well enough to keep that IV out of the room. I spend a few contractions on top of the bed in discomfort, and ask to go back in the tub. The pain is at least cut in half when my belly is immersed.

At what must be transition I say to Julie, "Maybe we ought to talk about drugs now." She says, "I don't think so." Shortly after that I feel the first urge to push. I get out of the tub, onto the bed, and Clara confirms that indeed I am at ten centimeters. I smile, another triumph. My body knows how to open. Here is proof that I can make it through the first stage of labor, given the chance.

The first pushes are not effective, Clara says because the bag of waters is cushioning the baby's head which still slightly floats. She says I could continue until the waters break or the baby moves down spontaneously, or she could break the waters. I say to break them, knowing that with the cervix already open, there are fewer drawbacks to this procedure. She does, and water gushes out of me, splashes Clara, and again I smile. Lots of water! This baby was not postmature, this baby had had lots of water to swim and be nestled in. Waves of satisfaction sweep through me, and then there is intense, knife-like pain and I yell, "What are you doing?" Nothing, they are doing nothing. The baby merely took a plunge through the cervix as the waters left, clearing the way for the uterine pressure to do its work.

Meconium is present, which means I will now wear an external monitor during pushing. They agree to turn the sound off of the monitor at my request, and I gracefully acquiesce to the belt. I feel confident that this will be the only prop or intervention necessary.

I quickly develop a routine; one foot is on Michael's shoulder, the other on Julie's, so I push with knees bent, my back propped by pillows. I have no desire or need to squat, as plenty is happening without a perpendicular angle to maximize gravity. I know when to push—it is an uncontrollable urge, and I growl as my body doubles over, and feel the baby move down me. Then I rest; between contractions there is no pain, I am aware of movement in the room—someone wheeling in a baby warmer, Clara saying, "We're going to have a baby here soon." The room is still dark, and a spotlight is set up at the foot of the bed so Clara can see. I think, How strange, I haven't been in a spotlight since a junior high production of *My Fair Lady.*

The baby is moving quickly, and I hear a nurse exclaim, "She's so strong! Built like a Mac Truck!" Clara tugs at the perineum. The familiar twinge of it stretching does not disturb me as we have been doing perineal massage for weeks. After the next contraction Clara grabs my left hand and puts it between my legs so I can feel the baby's head emerging. I feel something with the texture of a wet walnut, and take my hand off in surprise. Two more gentle pushes and the head is crowning. Then the head emerges, Clara begins suctioning, and asks, "Who wants to cut the cord?" I say I want to, and she says, "Due to the meconium we'll have to bypass that nicely." One more push, and the body propels out of me. He is out on the bed, the cord is cut, and I get a glimpse of a baby so big there are folds of fat at his little ankles. I can't believe a baby so big could come out of me. Another triumph! A neonatologist checks him as he gustily cries. I whimper while Clara works on me to get the placenta out. I keep saying, "It hurts too much." When they bring him to me, I feel no more pain. He is all the analgesic I need. Clara does three stitches from a small tear—not bad, for pushing out a nine-and-a-half-pound, twenty-three-inch-long baby. I put him immediately to the breast. A nurse takes a picture of Michael, Julie, me, and the baby, and I have the biggest smile on my face.

Like transparencies covering me and the room, my first son's birth and my miscarriage are present. We are all lighter, at a higher frequency. Later that day I realize that my second son Kyle was born on October fifth, and the miscarried baby was born and died a year ago on October sixth. I have no conscious chance to mourn her this year, as I am immersed in new life.

This second birth was terrific, lovely, wonderful. In many ways I was satisfied and could move on. Yet it did not and could not have the power to keep my first son's birth from impacting my past, present, or future. I do not expect, and would not want it to.

INDIVIDUALIZED NEEDS

A woman's needs during a subsequent birth are entirely individual. I needed the safety net of a hospital birth due to the experience of a prolapsed cord requiring immediate intervention. Though there was minimal risk of a repeat occurrence, my fear required the hospital setting. I was very careful in choosing both the hospital and the caregivers, and had an optimal experience. I wanted to be in a birthing room in the way it was meant to be used. I wanted to be able to walk down the hospital hallway happy, able to wheel my own baby into the nursery so I could take a break for a shower. I wanted to cocoon myself, have the sheets changed for me. I needed to exert my influence to receive the desired care that provided a safe environment for birth. I am still amazed that I pushed a baby out; my body still sings with joy.

Some women are so loyal to their doctors that though they were not satisfied with a previous birth, they continue to receive the same treatment. There are many different ways to seek security and to maintain a relationship with a doctor; to give him or her another chance is a respectable choice. Whatever decision helps a woman feel safe is what she needs to do.

Knowing there are choices to be made is key. Small-town residents often do not realize there are other options; yet I have heard of women driving two hundred miles to receive different obstetrical care.

When Vicky became pregnant for the second time, she first tried to find a medical doctor or certified nurse-midwife practice who would support her goal of a noninterventive VBAC. She could not find anyone who did not place restrictions on labor practices that she considered unreasonable. Merely considering a hospital or contact with a doctor brought back such vivid memories of trauma that she was not able to cope with this approach. She decided to use lay midwives and have her second baby at home. Her husband Greg provided support for going in this direction, and they found a team of three lay midwives who agreed to provide prenatal as well as labor and delivery care. Here is Vicky's description of her second pregnancy and birth.

> I had a lot of anxieties when I was pregnant with Lara, and one of the main fears was that I wouldn't have her vaginally after having such a big mouth about things. I told everybody that the first cesarean shouldn't have happened and that I couldn't handle going through that again. There was no way that I could imagine there being a *real* need for a c-section. The only way I could think about it is that the same exact thing could happen again. The same rape. And I don't think that everybody's c-sections are like rape, whether

they're necessary or not. But all I could think about was this horrible thing happening again.

It was a very conscious effort for me to heal enough before Lara's birth, it didn't just happen. I really had to consciously say, I don't want to live like this any more. Even though the first birth happened the way it did I had to somehow rise above it. Like Greg had said, "Are you going to let him [the doctor] ruin us, too?" That statement hit home, especially when I got pregnant again. I knew I had to get it together. So, it was a very conscious effort. Nothing from the experience has gone away on its own, nothing, not one ounce of it. I think it was my inner strength that got me through. I didn't want to be consumed by the past. I had to make the choice about whether to let the past situation ruin my life or not. It has permanently affected me in a lot of ways, I'll never be the same. But now there's hope. When the cesarean first happened, I thought there was no way I was ever going to be able to handle anything. Now it's changed, by reading and talking to people, and praying a lot.

With Lara's birth, all through the entire delivery it was like I gave birth to two babies. I would do things for both of them. For the birth of me and for her. I would never again go to a doctor for a birth. I tried to find one I could work with, but I couldn't, I thought I would die. I asked a lot of people and found these three midwives. Emily, Julie, and Sarah. They were great, they talked to Greg and me about the things that mattered. I knew I could trust them to help me have my baby on my own. They asked me at each visit what I dreamed about. They knew how I felt about Dr. Harvey. They knew I'd rather die than have that happen again. So I guess I was prepared when I went into my second labor. My waters broke first.

The midwives never checked me during my labor with Lara, so I don't know if I froze at the same point as when Dr. Harvey did the c-section the first time. I could not relax, I was freaked out, I was hyper, I could not get in control of myself. I was just a total crazed woman through that labor. I was all over the house. I was almost embarrassed. I could not shut my mouth, I never shut up. Then I was to the point, it must have been transition, and said, "You have to check me," and one of my midwives, Emily, said, "Vicky, we can't check you, your waters broke, and you could get infected." I said, "I don't care, take your chances, use your sterile gloves, you have to check me." So they checked me, and they said, "She's at about seven." I had to push, and I said, "I thought this was over." And then Julie must have seen the look on my face, and she said, "And oh, it's Thursday, and Dr. Harvey's on call." And I said, "I have to push." They said, "No, you can't, you're only at seven." I said,

"No, I'm at ten." and less than ten minutes later my daughter was born. I didn't tear at all, and she came out all at once, because she came so suddenly. But I didn't tear. I got to hold her right afterwards. Kind of the ending and the beginning all at once. I had a lot to work through during that birth, and I don't know what exactly happened, but it was really empowering.

I felt so good, I was out swinging Jack two hours later. I mean, I was tired from no sleep, but I can't really describe it. It was really great.

There are no words to describe what her birth did for me. It's almost selfish to say, because it was her birth, but it was mine, too. A rebirth, because I really had died after my c-section. I would always say to Greg, "I'm dead inside. I love you and the baby, but I'm dead." I used to be such a nice person, but now I'm not. My girlfriend said when she called from the hospital when she was having her baby, "The nurses won't let me walk around during labor." I said to her, "Won't let you? Do they tie you down to the chair? How do they not let you do that?" I've become so—so mean, doctors hate me now, well, some doctors do.

I've always had this fairy tale life, things had always gone my way, I was this, I was that, I was everything, and something happened to her. Now at least I'm alive again.

Vicky created a safe environment that allowed her to experience birth naturally, forcefully, and with joy. She had the support of caregivers who understood her past birth experience. They did not belittle it or try to talk her into a compromise such as "trying for a VBAC" at the hospital. Vicky knew what she needed in order to feel safe, relaxed, and strong. This enabled her to successfully birth her second baby.

By recognizing previous traumas, Vicky and I had much greater chances for success. Obviously our styles and choices were different, and well suited to our individual needs. Instead of freezing in a memory of a past birth, there was fluidity—Vicky uncontrollably talked and moved about her house throughout her labor while she worked out her feelings. In a hospital bathtub, I floated silently, saying only "Now" so my labor coach, Julie, would begin the affirmation which brought me through the tunnel of labor.

The common ground Vicky and I shared included identifying our fears, carefully planning for the delivery, and having several supportive people help us through the birth process. We each had many options with which to work.

Ellen's story of her subsequent birth in the previous chapter is just as powerful in its healing ability; she was not traumatized from the necessary medical interventions or her vastly altered expectations.

She was involved in the decision making, she was well informed, and she knew what was needed for healing afterwards. Her wisdom grew; she knows she can trust herself, she knows who to turn to for a compassionate and friendly ear, and she knows the power of birth.

Regardless of the choices made or the outcome, a subsequent birth is a wellspring of blessings.

FOR WORK ON YOUR OWN

Question One: What are your fears of a past birth repeating itself? Have you spoken with someone about them?

Question Two: If you have decided to have another baby, in what ways are your plans different from the first birth? In what ways are they similar to the first birth? Do you believe there is a need for different plans?

FOR FURTHER READING

Though the following books are particularly useful, a perusal of the entire reference section is recommended. Books selected depend on which particular issues couples bring to a subsequent birth.

Cohen, Nancy Wainer, and Estner, Lois. (1983) *Silent Knife: Cesarean Prevention and Vaginal Birth after Cesarean (VBAC)*. Westport, CT: Bergin & Garvey.
Jones, Carl. (1988) *The Birth Partner's Handbook*. Minneapolis, MN: Meadowbrook.
Kitzinger, Sheila. (1987) *Your Baby, Your Way: Making Pregnancy Decisions and Birth Plans*. New York: Pantheon.
Panuthos, Claudia, and Romeo, Catherine. (1984) *Ended Beginnings: Healing Childbearing Losses*. New York: Warner Books.
Peterson, Gayle. (1991) *An Easier Childbirth: A Workbook for Pregnant Women*. Los Angeles: Jeremy Tarcher Press.
Richards, Lynn Baptisti. (1987) *Vaginal Birth after Cesarean*. Westport, CT: Bergin & Garvey.
Simkin, Penny. (1989) *The Birth Partner: Everything You Need to Know to Help a Woman through Childbirth*. Boston: Harvard Common Press.

FEELINGS, THOSE SUCKERS

"No, no, not feelings, anything but those."

"I'd rather dig my own basement with my bare hands than know how I feel."

"Every time I see a pregnant woman I ache inside, knowing she might have the kind of birth I wished for."

"I don't believe in crying over spilt milk. What's done is done. What good is it to dig into all this now?"

"I want to move on, I'm so tired of dealing with all this. I wish it were over once and for all. Why can't I just forget about it?"

"Feelings, feelings, feelings. I'm so sick of feelings. Just shut up about this anger crap—who said I was angry? If you would just stop trying to tell me how I'm angry, I'd be fine."

"My husband doesn't have any problem with the birth—he has never cried, never felt the loss I feel, and I don't feel free to tell him any of this. But once I found myself with a knife in the kitchen, wondering how easily it would cut my arm. That's when I knew I'd better talk to someone."

"I don't have any more feelings about my baby's birth, I'm done with that part of healing. I cried when I came home from the hospital, but since then everything's been fine."

"I'm terrified of getting pregnant again. I don't think I could live through another c-section, I would just want to die on the table. I don't know how anyone can go through giving birth again, I'd rather walk on hot coals."

"Why did this have to happen to me?"

Every feeling about birth matters, no matter how long that feeling lasts or what it is about, no matter how unreasonable, irrational, or out of proportion it seems. Any feeling, no matter how strong, is easier to live with once it is named. Naming creates edges so the feeling is only as big as the room or the city or the sky, and not bigger than the entire universe. But to experience this kind of relief requires a leap of faith, an abandonment into feelings, an embracement that goes against many creeds. Now that the pain is recognized, a woman can take this leap and begin to voice her feelings about how her birth occurred. But does she want to?

This chapter focuses on the need to release fear, grief, anger, whining, and joy as well as when to take breaks from feelings. Each emotion released has different characteristics. After a woman embraces her feelings when she is ready to, the birth can be accepted as it happened. Once acceptance has begun, forgiveness and change are possible, though not always required.

Each feeling is discussed separately, for anger is different from fear, which is different from joy, which is different from grief. Many times a woman's feelings are actually mixed, as though different watercolors have bled together on wet paper. Sometimes the blue hues predominate, yet other colors are present, peeking out from underneath, encroaching on the corners, or radiating out from the center. Sometimes feelings change depending on the level of awareness. Keep in mind that traits of one feeling may apply to another. Aspects of what is learned about fear can be applied to anger, and vice versa. In order to understand each feeling and relate it specifically toward giving birth, each feeling is discussed separately. First, suppression of all feelings is discussed.

SUPPRESSION OF FEELINGS

No matter what the feeling, if suppressed, it will become stronger. Feelings have lives of their own. It is natural to wish to avoid pain. An intense feeling is painful, can cause a woman to feel as though she will die. But when a feeling is knocking on her door, it will not go away, no matter how deeply it is buried.

Stuffing feelings will make them stronger, and they will emerge in less constructive, uncontrollable ways. If someone says, "I will not feel this way. I will have a good day, I am not going to be depressed," that effort will boomerang. She may stuff her face, drink, watch television, or be active, attempting to numb herself. Then her feeling will show up as twenty or thirty pounds carried around on the outside of her, or she may have no creativity, no energy for living—because it all is going toward keeping that feeling "under control." This approach is costly, and may lead several years later toward medication for depression, neglect of her children, or undefined sharpness toward anyone in her path.

Sometimes one feeling is used to suppress another. Tears may flow easily but anger may never be expressed. Conversely, anger may be easily accessed but fear and grief unknown. If there is a short range of feelings experienced, for example, if anger is consistently felt and nothing else, then it is worth asking about the other feelings. Are they present underneath the anger? Has the woman ever grieved for the lost birth of her dreams? Has she felt rage toward the hospital? Has she ever known her fear of being cut, her fear of death? Or if sadness is only felt and she cries and never yells, she can ask the same question: what is underneath her tears? A red-hot lava bed? Black fear? Rage so intense it scares her, so she cries instead?

Yet to let feelings follow their courses, wind their ways out of her, can feel as threatening as a loaded gun at her head. This is not a joke. To sit with a big feeling, no matter what it is—anger, sadness, fear—can feel lethal. However, I have never heard of a feeling killing someone, even though it can appear that strong. A feeling is dangerous when it is unacknowledged and suppressed. For example, lack of awareness of rage means it is more likely to be expressed unexpectedly, violently. A new mother who talks about rage and expresses her hate and desire for destruction is less likely to be violent. I never heard of a desire for revenge hurting someone else. The act of revenge is destructive, not the desire or the feeling of rage preceding it. This dynamic is also true for self-hate and self-destruction. Suppression of feelings is costly.

A woman may believe she is going to die as the feeling rolls through her, but she won't. The trick is to sit with the feeling until this intensity, this sensation of death passes, and light is perceived at the end of the tunnel. Get help with this waiting period if necessary; support can help. Then what is left is strength, knowledge of the self, and confidence that one can feel so intensely and survive. A woman feels what is underneath, the self-confidence, depth, and simultaneously the excruciating and exhilarating sense of life and death.

Experiencing feelings is not easy, and they rarely all arise at once. After feeling blind rage or red-hot anger, after facing fears or recognizing losses and deciding there is nothing further to lose, a woman may be sprawled and spent. But her feelings have changed, because she expressed them.

When a woman feels rotten, and there is nowhere to go but up, it is time to release and let go. When she's hit bottom, there is no longer the fear of falling. Now it can only get better. A vacuum is created in her emotional universe, and mystery may be waiting to fill it. This process may occur slowly and methodically, or very fast and explosively. The direction toward releasing and knowing emotions is what is essential. Then the tunnel will be traversed. This passage will forever remain a part of her, but she will emerge at the other end.

This emergence is the mystery, and it is what is impossible to imagine while lying on the near side of giving in to the pain, the anger, the terror, or the grief. On the other side lies what any survivor of trauma will affirm, the awareness that the universe is great enough to include both the loss and the gain. Tentative steps are taken as a woman emerges out of the tunnel.

Anyone who has recovered from trauma will confirm that healing does not mean that the past and related feelings are buried and gone. They are not forever out of a woman's mind, never to bother her again. Healing is feeling the presence of the traumatic experience at its own place at the banquet table, amongst all the other guests. It is amongst the good times, the other children, friends, accomplishments, and even the wonderful births. Another leaf is placed in the table to accommodate all the guests, for no one is banished. That is the irony of knowing oneself. It is knowing all the parts—not just the good, powerful, pretty parts, but the nasties, the failures, the bad dreams, the terrifying moments. Imagine setting a place at the table for the birth a woman wishes had happened differently. Let that image in. Then anger at needing to put out this effort may also surface. Or fear. Or grief. Or joy.

ALLOWING FEELINGS TO BE EMBRACED

Fear

Fear is a natural, protective response to threat. When unexpected outcomes or trauma are involved in birth, often there is real or perceived threat, and fear is felt. Afterwards, if she is in a safe environment, the woman can decompress her fear and know that now she is safe. She trusts her inner sense of the difference between feeling safe and feeling fear. When the threats associated with birth are acknowledged, whether medically induced or not, a woman has more effective and immediate opportunities to heal.

Fear is twofold. There is the memory of fear if painful events happened, if the baby or mother was in danger or threatened with danger during labor and delivery. This residual fear may be stored in a woman's body, trapped because she won't acknowledge its existence in the first place. It is too scary to acknowledge the fear, and this keeps the fear alive.

Second, a woman may be afraid of a future event based on her disempowering experience during birth. She may have walked into a hospital confident and optimistic, then been tied down and had her body violated in many unexpected ways. Fear is born out of the chance for further abuse, out of future times when she may not have the resources to protect herself. She is afraid of becoming vulnerable again. Or afraid of further loss if hers or the baby's health was compromised or if life was taken. Concrete evidence exists that bad things can happen, not only to her body, but to her precious baby.

A woman fears she will not have the strength to stand up for herself or bear further loss. She may face another doctor who tells her she must have a vacuum extraction delivery, drugs, or a preventive cesarean due to whatever reasons. The fear hits her in the face worse than a doctor could. "I am not strong enough to fight this man or woman. I do not know how to get myself out of this. I am a child in front of a big person, powerless." She retreats into herself, becomes small, compliant, and powerless.

Fear may be felt yet undefined, because people around her act as though everything went fine during the birth, giving her the old "What is important is your baby is healthy, there's nothing to be upset about" message. It induces a particular fear of being crazy. A woman is told that she is safe, that everything was done during the birth to make sure she and the baby were safe, yet she still feels her heart pound in her chest and ears. She attempts to hide her fear from herself and others, pretending to be something she is not. Because this fear isn't even supposed to exist, how can she possibly describe it or put edges around it?

Sometimes getting away from the usual routines or environment helps a woman discover what is going on. Driving only twenty minutes out of town works for some individuals. Getting a sitter and finding a place to do whatever needs to be done is a very valuable investment, whether a woman needs to mine her feelings, assess her goals about any aspect of her life, or take a nap. Vicky spontaneously had this experience when she drove with her family out of state. This was the first time since childbirth that she had been further away from home than the store or visiting friends. Vicky described what happened when she was about six hours away from home.

Jack was about two and a half months old, and it really hit me—before, I just felt terrible and was depressed about my birthing experience. But the reality hit me about what actually happened, the whole thing. I was sitting in the car, Greg was driving and listening to his music, and the whole event replayed, how really awful it was. I had been dealing with the birth for two and a half months, and for the first time saw it in a totally different light. I was fucked over big time. I was, no matter what anybody else said. I said, "Greg, pull over," and I was just sobbing, that this had really happened to me. That was the first time it felt real. Before I felt anger and was upset and weepy, but that was the first real attack. I knew I needed to get my reactions under control before I got pregnant again.

It didn't make me feel any better, it was just the same pain over and over. I've never experienced feeling anything like that before. I couldn't duplicate it, my body was in terror, total terror. I thought it would never end.

I might have been in shock before then. I had never been away from my house except to shop. I had never gone anywhere else, because I was recovering, and trying to get used to a new baby. That was the first time I had ever been so far away from the actual physical situation. I was six hours away in the car, and not around all these people who were always stuffing what really happened. It was the first chance for the whole birth experience to start coming out. I suppose finally feeling it all was better than being resentful and trying to believe other people telling me that I should be so grateful.

This was the beginning of Vicky's reconciliation with what really happened to her. She was afraid her intense feelings would last forever, but they did subside. The amount and intensity of feelings is usually underrated; yet with every recognition of feelings, opportunity exists to clear them out. Releasing her feelings was more beneficial than being resentful, or telling herself she should be so grateful, or worrying that she was crazy. At first, Vicky's feelings seemed much larger than herself; as she acknowledged them, they took up less and less of her universe. They became more manageable.

The story might need telling and the terror or anger felt many more times than originally expected. As I wrote this chapter, I came upon a book that stated that 50 percent of babies born with prolapsed cords don't make it. I remembered my traumatic experience again. I am sure I've read that statistic before, but it immediately took me back to my terror of my baby dying. But the terror doesn't overwhelm me anymore; it's just a part of me. It's just there. Edges exist around this fear, both because of my recognition that there was risk involved and because it is a past event, not part of my current world.

Without edges, the fear feels bigger than it really is; it can feel as big as the continent. When edges are put around the fear, a woman knows what sort of demon she is struggling with. She knows how much of the sky is actually filled with her fear, how much of the room or the couch, or whatever size and shape the fear takes on. The color of fear, its density, all its physical characteristics can be imagined. This further helps to define the fear. An actual picture of the fear can be created or only imagined in the mind's eye.

Now her fear is identified. Here is her dread. It is not the whole world. Look, the rest of the sky is blue, the rest of the room is safe and warm. The fear is there, safety is here. Edges have been created. When another look is taken at the fear, it becomes smaller, because more safety has been created by talking about it.

Another way to put edges around fear is to define its detailed characteristics. If a woman experiences a fear of all doctors after a traumatic birth or hospital experience, then her fear feels as huge as the sky or the world. If she can identify more specific characteristics of her fear, then she may discover that she is afraid of a doctor who will not listen to her, who will not acknowledge mistakes, or who will withhold information of what is about to occur. Then she knows her fear. She has information about what kind of medical attention to seek from a future doctor; she can seek one who will treat her the way she wants to be treated, or treat her child or other family members accordingly. Knowing her fear gives her information. Then she will walk into a subsequent doctor's office feeling all her fear, yet knowing this event may not deserve all that fear. A good litmus test for herself is to ask if perhaps her response or feeling is much bigger than the current event. If so, then a portion—sometimes a large portion—of the response or feeling belongs to the past. If the response is then directed toward the past, the present becomes more manageable. A woman can have her son's ingrown toenail treated without the entire sky falling down upon her; she can separate the current situation from the previous trauma.

Grief

The birth of any child is an introduction to loss on two levels. First, giving birth to someone so loved creates more risk of loss, and second, the birth outcome is beyond anyone's ultimate control. When trauma occurs, the lesson that a woman cannot control her own body or life or her child's life becomes real in a matter of minutes or hours.

The universal aspect of loss associated with childbirth includes loss of the pregnancy, loss of child-free lives, loss of dream babies and births, loss of sleep—any new mother could write her own list.

Grieving those losses for me was bittersweet, like wishing I could go back to a favorite place for vacation, or wishing I could recapture a past event in my life.

There is a darker side to the grief over the loss of control, of safety, of innocence and trust, in something once held sacrosanct. Before giving birth, I had images of smiling faces, pink nighties, and a trip home from the hospital with a bundle of joy. My naivete and innocence are symptoms of our society's portrayal of birth, a portrayal that creates a handicap. I was a well-educated and informed individual, yet I trusted beyond reason what the medical establishment was capable of. At age thirty-four, my first son's birth was an initiation into my loss of innocence. For some time, any vestige of false hope was gone, as was my basic trust in life.

This loss creates a wall of grief difficult to define because it is made up of intangible pieces; no one has died. Instead, ideals, values, and trust have died. Birth fantasies and expectations, unrealistic or otherwise, also have died and need to be grieved.

After my second child, born so relatively calmly and wonderfully, other types of losses were faced. Several months after his birth I was hit with the enormity of my attachment to him. My fear of loss had to be reckoned with. This may sound strange, but I had to grieve the potential loss of my child, because my fear of losing him was so great. I had to face up to the reality that his life was not a certainty; I had birthed him successfully, but the rest of the time I had with him was up for grabs.

As I sorted through my worst fears, I grieved another lost innocence. After my first birth, the basic loss of innocence was hidden in trauma. After my second birth, I was hit again with the uncertainty factor faced with any child. I had naively thought that a good, safe birth would carry me through the next twenty or thirty years.

A traumatic birth is like baptism in fire about a basic aspect of being a mother: no matter what a woman does, she cannot guarantee her child's safety. Birth is experienced as the door between life and death. If a woman has not previously experienced a major loss, such as the death of someone close, or another major upheaval, then birth may widely open her eyes. The uncertainty of birth is rarely discussed; to acknowledge whatever loss occurred during the birth of her baby provides an outlet for her grief. A miscarriage, a cesarean, hoping for a girl and having a boy, or any baby who has died no matter how long its life—all these births require grieving, and memories will always be with a mother.

Tears pour over the birth a woman hoped for that did not happen. They pour over the baby who was planned for that didn't arrive.

Sorrow is felt for innocence lost with respect to the perception of the world as a safe place and the idea that babies are supposed to be born amidst love, not fear. Sadness prevails as a woman's body embodies pain and betrayal and she mistrusts her sense of who can be trusted. Grief is present after the birth when there are so few willing ears to hear her story, especially the lack of familial ears. Friends turn away. A new mother finds herself alone, seeking safety in a closet, bingeing on food, watching television. She grieves and shows it by rarely leaving the house with her new baby.

Grief is the acknowledgment that loss is part of life, that a woman's world includes this pain of separation, and possibly the pain of existence. Grief is a huge reconciliation with loss. There are many individual ways to express grief. Some women immediately pour it out. Others remain in shock or disbelief for long periods. The loss, like fear, can seem bigger than the world, and it often takes concerted effort to discover that the universe also includes joy and life.

Grief often appears to be depression, as a woman sorts through her personal muck to find this hidden life. Her life, when she is grieving, is truly shrouded. She needs to gather evidence that there is life worth seeking. Gathered fragments of this evidence may be thin at first. Persistence in seeking a light-filled, loving corner is necessary to rebuild what has been shattered. These efforts are cumulative. First she may hear a woman's story of a lousy birth followed by a wonderful affirmation of new motherhood, another's story of her second birth at home after an unnecessary cesarean, or news of new legislation in a far-away state giving traditional midwives the same authority as a doctor to greet new life into the world. She may tentatively touch her scar, accepting it as a permanent part of her body, appreciating the healing power that has closed the wound and protects all of her. She may feel certain that if she ever gives birth again, she will avoid the disfiguring, painful, lumpy two-pronged episiotomy. She now knows she was not responsible for the doctor who cut her, for she did not put the scissors in his or her hand.

Any event or story, or an accumulation of incidents, can allow a glimmer of light to be seen or hope to be felt. These slender threads become stronger, and alongside grief, joy becomes once more possible.

There are few advantages to advertising birth solely as a joyous, pain-free event. In the case of grief, it is doubly damaging. A woman expects to feel love, pleasure, and satisfaction with her baby's arrival. Instead, her trust is shattered, and she feels loss and sorrow over whatever aspect of birth the trauma has upended.

Anger

Angry statements I often hear include: "It is impossible to tell you how I feel inside—you know maybe 20 percent. It's indescribable. I am so mad, I could fuel a semi across the country three times with my anger, and still have enough left over to explode myself into oblivion."

"Anger, anger, anger, anger. I am so angry still about what happened. I want fire breath I can direct toward that doctor. I want him to suffer. I was never a vengeful person, but I just want him to know what he did to me."

"There is no way for me to get all this anger out, so I might as well move on. It will never go away, so why try to get rid of it? It's too painful to focus on it any more."

Anger is the most power-producing emotion. It fuels an individual to take action, make changes, plow through mountains if she desires. It's as though invisible hands push and pull, as though a strong wind blows through her, and she learns to appreciate the raw force. Anger, once turned inward and now flowing outward, creates a whole different perspective.

When I am angry about being mistreated, I have the energy to change doctors, day cares, relationships. It enables me to say what I want, gather materials or information together, and decide to stay or leave. Whatever action needs to occur then occurs. Anger is a gift of energy. When I am angry about a miserable circumstance, I use that energy to vacuum, throw things out, get things done. I write the letter or make the call that clarifies what I am or am not responsible for and make known what someone else needs to know about me. When I am angry, I am definitely awake.

Anger is perceived as threatening because so often it is experienced as cruelty or violence. Fear may exist that a tail of violence is attached to anger. That anger will swipe out to destroy and hurt, it will beat up somebody. Indiscriminate or ill-meant anger is terrifying, and I do not advocate its use. I am describing the expression of anger that is valuable in its ability to provide energy for taking care of oneself. When I am angry, I am ready to defend, to smash what needs to be smashed so there is room for what is new or good. Anger can take a woman where she needs to go next. She will be able to run a marathon if needed, be able to get out of her pit of despair and make changes.

I was unspeakably angry after the birth of my first son, outraged that I was cut open and felt misery, that he had been at risk, that I did not deliver vaginally. The following months and years involved chipping away this anger, flake by flake.

When Evan was eleven months old, I took my first trip without him. I expected to relax in the sun and have a break, but unexpectedly, this geographical distance allowed for a huge flake of anger to fly off.

I had never been separated from Evan overnight, but to my surprise, when the opportunity came, I jumped at it. A friend offered me a free place to stay in Tucson for a week with a free plane ticket. The opportunity was too good to pass up.

After a few tears in the airport while saying good-by and seeing other babies, boarding the plane was a lot easier than I expected. I left Evan with his father, secretly glad Michael would be alone with his eleven-month-old son, having to provide all the care for awhile. I wanted Michael to appreciate me more.

My resentment was so huge. I wish it was different, that I could have gladly nursed Evan until he was two, could have been less self-centered, and could have appreciated Michael's efforts more, but I couldn't. I needed a lot of room to scream and yell, let off steam, find out there was a life besides my boxed in existence of living month to month. As soon as I boarded that plane, thoughts of Evan and Michael almost vanished. I walked down the aisle and found my seat next to a woman holding an eight-month-old. I looked around for an empty seat anywhere else, and there were none. Sitting by that infant made the landing more remarkable, more like truly getting away—finally, from babies and anything to do with them. I stepped off the plane and shook off babies for good.

In early March, the weather was hot and sunny in Tucson, with mild winds. Every day I swam in the streams, soaked up desert sun, and took hikes along mountain trails while my thoughts roamed. Visions of anger dances came to me, and I danced them. *A tall, lanky stick figure of firey red with a black face jigs down the mountain trail of brown-red desert rock. Energy streams from her fingers, spidery webs of gold. Toxins of anger exude out of every pore. Cleansing water pours into her mouth, down her throat, pours through her, floating through every cell.*

I kept yelling on the trails, kept waking every morning feeling anger, kept writing in my journal every day of vicious thoughts, hateful phrases, I hated my life, hated the dilemma of loving my child but hating what we had been through this past year. I went to dinner with my friend and spent two hours describing my anger toward Michael, toward my scar, toward wanting another baby but hating any mention of birth at the same time.

By the end of the week, I had barely begun to relax, and could have used more time to get rid of even more anger, more tension.

Talking with Michael on the phone, I said, "You know, I don't even miss you, I'm really surprised." Silence on the other end; I wasn't very tactful.

"You know what I mean. I'm doing so much by myself here, I'm not filled up yet. I'll be glad to see you and Evan, but it feels so good to be away."

When I got off the plane I *was* glad to see them and be reunited as a family. Michael stood there holding Evan in his blue corduroy overalls, his chubby baby face lit up, and Evan's arms reached out as Michael's did, for me to hold them.

Obviously my inhibitions dropped when I was in a different environment, in an experience similar to Vicky's when she drove out of town. And appropriately, I vented while away from a vulnerable baby and from a husband who did not deserve all of the rage and anger that anyone in my path would have received. Michael and I had many fights as we negotiated a marriage after birth, but much of my anger needed to be dealt with by me alone. After that Tucson trip, I learned my lesson well, and tended to any angry bubbles needing to surface so that such an extreme release was not necessary. The lanky red fiery figure will always be part of me; I respect her and love her. She visits as needed, rather than exploding onto the scene.

Vicky's anger was initially consuming, then became constructive at a later time.

I had such hate, if I had a machine gun and I weren't worried about going to jail, I would love to go up there and just shoot people on the birth floor. Every doctor or nurse I could find. My mother said, "Don't say that, people will think you're crazy, and if anything happens they'll come looking for you."

I'm mean now when I go to the hospital to visit my grandma. Not mean, but I say what she needs, and why isn't that being done, I question everything. Whereas before I would have been nice, like would you please check if she needs a clean gown? Last year Greg was in the hospital for kidney stones. I'm sure I just drove them nuts in the emergency room. Are you sure that's the right medicine, may I see the bottle? Now would you please put on gloves to administer the shot, because I really don't want your blood mixing with my husband's. I went on and on.

Though she sometimes struggles with bitterness about the need for protection, Vicky now knows how to protect and act on behalf of herself and her family.

Blame. Rarely does a woman not blame herself, even if outwardly she holds the medical establishment or other entity responsible. She wonders what she did, how the fabric of her being drew such a lousy experience to her. No matter what emotional or physical wounds exist, a woman takes the opportunity to blame herself, for she is her easiest target. Blame, because she has failed as a woman to perform this most womanly act of birthing her baby with the power of her own body. Even if intervention saved a life. Even though she did the best she could with what she had.

Blame is an attitude, not even a feeling, and needs to be distinguished from accountability. It may smoulder as guilt, an ever-present excuse for self-doubt. Blame is a mind-set against someone, and it does not empower. Blame sits on the edges of rage, for if a woman acted out her blame, either against herself or others, she would tear herself or others limb from limb. She would blow up the hospital, blow up the baby for being born in the way he or she was born; she would annihilate all doctors. Whatever scenario a woman has for her blame, she would destroy. She would be left with destruction, and very little with which to rebuild. Rebuild what? What, says a woman, could I possibly want to build out of this dung heap? Life is not fair, says the whiner, who sneaks in at every opportunity.

Whining

Fall arrived, and Evan could sit up by himself. Time was going by, and I was still trying to figure out how the birth trauma could have been prevented and what was wrong with me that caused it to happen. Even though the birth was one of the most wonderful things that ever happened, this whiner hung on.

I struggled longer than I like to admit with my whining side, with perceiving myself as a hapless victim, flip-flopping between self-blame that I should have been able to change what happened and wishing that a power much, much greater and all-caring than myself had rescued me from my own personal version of a tar pit.

Whining is volatile and can be a reflection of depression, tiny power, and being stuck. Though not a feeling, it is a way of expressing feelings. "Why did this have to happen to me? I'm always learning the hard way, why couldn't it be easy this time? If I were lucky like my friend Louise, I could be happy like her."

On the positive side, whining is often confused with complaining. Complaining is an effective antidote to denial; when a situation sucks, it needs to be acknowledged. The following is complaining:

I hate winter.
I hate the way my baby was born.
I hate having old clothes.
I hate the shape of my tush.
I am sick and tired of getting up every night every two hours.
I can't stand this heat, I will suffocate in this room unless that
    window is opened.
I will not eat another green vegetable ever again, for as long as I
    live. I have force-fed myself broccoli, and I will gag. Get it out
    of my sight until I say so.

Complaining is a stepping stone toward acceptance, for once I
have realized what I don't like or what I wish were different, then I
have the ability to choose to live with what I have or change it. I also
have more ability to state what I do like and what I want. This perspective is much different from wishing something had never happened. The following is whining:

Why does it have to be so cold?
Why does it have to be so hot?
He's always picking on me.
He never drives fast enough.
She always gets to use the bathroom first.
Why did this have to happen to me?
What did I do to deserve this?
I made such good plans, this shouldn't have happened.
I can't face this, bad things always happen to me.
I'll never heal from this experience.
My son will be damaged for life, I know it.

At face value, and when in its depths, whining appears to have no
solution. Since the regret exists, how can a woman change history? She
can't. Whining is wishing it weren't so.
    Think of a whining child, demanding attention by not asking
directly but just maintaining a drone of demands. "But you said you
would, I want water, she has water. Why can't I have the same glass?
I wanted the good water, you got it out of the tap, why can't I have it
out of the refrigerator? When you pour water for yourself, you get it
out of that special pitcher. I want cookies. . . "
    Imagine a child saying, "Mom, I don't like that water, would you
please get me the special water?" If I could, I'd get the special water for
a child asking so directly.
    Paradoxically, whining is often an expression of self-blame—try-

ing to figure out how I could have prevented something, if I'd only been somewhere else. It is also an expression of dependency. A whiner wants to be taken care of by someone else and not by herself.

There are few constructive responses to whining except to say, "Stop it." If a woman has phrases in her head like "Why did this have to happen to me?" or "Why can't it be different?" in the thousands of variations these can manifest themselves, then she could use the phrase "Stop it." She could see what terms of complaining she comes up with for the same content she was whining about. "Why did this happen to me?" could be transformed into "I hate that this happened to me." Another example: "If only I'd listened to my friend about that doctor, this would never have happened" metamorphoses into "I wish I'd listened to my friend, she was right. But here I am, having learned the hard way. Now what?"

Put whining in the present, for instance, during labor. First imagine a woman saying, "Why does it have to hurt so much?" Now imagine her saying, "I hate this pain." Or imagine a woman saying, "Why does this doctor want me to have so many drugs? There shouldn't be so many drugs." Then imagine her saying, "Would someone please rub my back? It makes the pain easier. No, I don't want any drugs." The second statement is much more powerful. It has substance that a medical practitioner would need to deal with. In the first case, the whining phrases could easily be ignored.

Unfortunately, whining is often a more socially acceptable behavior than outright dislike, anger, grief, complaining, or fear. Perhaps whining is the most common conduit for denial. In stating what she dislikes, acknowledging regret and her present circumstances, a woman steps toward acceptance of her life as it is. Then she can come up with choices about what she will do next.

Joy

To claim joy as a feeling is often no easier than claiming anger, sadness, fear, or anything else. Joy, happiness, gladness, pleasure—these are all ways to say that I am okay. I am enjoying my life. I deserve happiness.

One of the hidden benefits to acknowledging the other painful emotions is that pleasure is also accessed and felt. Feelings are a package deal. Hence the phrases: the agony and the ecstasy, the pain-pleasure principle, and no pain, no gain.

My most intense moments of joy are sometimes found after experiencing pain; there is a sharper, clearer sensation of joy. I know what joy feels like after I have been in despair.

My entire mother experience can be summed up with this contrast between joy and pain.

> I love my life, I hate my life. There is no way I would trade this experience, but it is so excruciating to be this tired, this stretched beyond my wildest fantasies of what it takes to be a parent. After being up half the night and meeting the demands of two kids, part of me wants to run screaming out into the four-foot snow drifts and head south. But the rest of me laughs and my body tingles with the excitement of being in the midst of these two growing little boys. I tire of the baby's demand to be held; he follows me, grabs my legs, and with my hands full of dirty dishes I am trapped in the middle of the kitchen floor. I shuffle to a counter, put down the dishes, and hold him. He snuggles in my arms—what could be better than this happiness? It is only strange in the context of doing a simple task such as the dishes, which becomes a two-hour ordeal.
>
> The last time Michael and I took a trip on our own, I could hardly wait for those three days of quiet, conversation, solitude, sleep. But what did we do as soon as we drove out of town? Talk about our kids, even about making another baby! How strange—I can't wait for a break away from my babies, and as soon as I leave I am infatuated with them.

I am confident similar dualities will spring up throughout my lifetime as a mother. When these babies came to our family my heart was opened. All the grief, fear, and anger make sense. I feel all of these because how else can I be so alive? Joy is now part of the package. I hope I always have access to all my feelings in order to be this alive. I love my life. I hate my life. And I am content.

Happiness for some means an absence of fear, a desire to be left alone: "Why can't I just have some peace?" If I push away fear, or turmoil, or anything, it becomes stronger. Once again, denial's potent disruption is felt, for denial also robs us of joy.

Go to a park. Observe which parents are waiting for an accident to happen, with a frown ready to spring forth. Observe which parents are enjoying the playground antics, either while pushing a child on the swing set or standing by as an observer. Notice their smiles and laughter. Imagine what is inhibiting others' laughter from bubbling up. My own satisfaction level has increased because I have claimed joy as my main purpose as a parent. Playing with a child is an ultimate high.

In the aftermath of unexpected birth events, joy is often well hidden, as the pain may be so great it needs to be focused on for a long time. Knowing that joy is present somewhere needs to be taken on faith. It will spring out in unexpected ways and places. After my first son's birth, when I felt despair, I was surprised also by the intensity of joy. It was as though the sunlight was more intense and the grass a more brilliant green, and the feel of my feet on the ground felt more solid than ever before.

Perhaps it is the realization that life is not always happy, life is not always sad, that makes intense joy possible. Standing in the middle allows me to see all the possibilities at once. When I am standing on the fulcrum, the balance point, my feet are constantly shifting to maintain the balance.

THE PATH TO RESOLUTION

Take Breaks from the Feelings

Some of the best advice ever given to me was to take a break from my own therapy. Don't work at healing all the time. Go do something frivolous, intellectual, or mundane. Give it a rest. I tend to sink my teeth into something and never let go. But my jaw gets tired, and so I followed this advice. I have applied it to many situations and projects, to any aspect of my life I am overworking.

Recovering from birth trauma or a related event is consuming; it can take up every waking and sleeping moment. Consider taking breaks. Commit to a conversation with a friend where birth is not mentioned. Go to a silly movie. Peel ten oranges and invite neighbors over to eat them. Take a bath and keep the mind empty.

It is natural to want to move through the healing journey as fast as possible; after all, who wants to be in pain or identify big feelings? "Let's get this over with," a woman says, and then is challenged by a much slower timetable, which her healing requires. A part of her may want to know what is buried inside and another part naturally wishes to block unpleasant feelings. If they are deeply buried, then she easily berates herself for having trouble facing them. Taking a break will help. An affirmation to use is: a woman remembers and finds her feelings and memories as she is ready to remember and find them.

Paradoxically, scheduling times to focus on feelings works for some women; then the rest of the day can go in other directions. Vicky did this with her husband. They scheduled time to talk and listen to one another, putting aside the subject of birth for the rest of the day. Their focus was on their relationship, which was also valuable. Work can be done alone or with a professional, whose office provides a safe place for an outpouring to occur. Any form of healing a woman is comfortable with is helpful; some massage therapists help to locate a feeling and provide ways to express it. Other women have friends, spiritual directors, or parenting groups to vent their feelings with. For some individuals, writing in a journal is a safe, effective outlet. Then when those planned hours or minutes are up, a woman can put the lid back on and resume her life.

The goal is to find balance, as in finding the middle point between joy and pain. Then a feeling is neither suppressed nor all-consuming. Give the feeling enough attention so that it is no longer a problem. Give the feeling a voice, so its message can be heard.

Regret

I sometimes regret certain episodes in my life, among them the way my first son was born. I still feel waves of jealousy when I hear of a similar labor that began like mine did but ended with a vaginal birth—the mother triumphant and bonded with her baby, her opportunity to heal more gently provided. Those regrets are futile, because my life is what it is. The gifts I was given with that first birth continue to pour through me. One important gift I received was the momentum to begin writing four years ago, producing this book and others.

I have known women who ten, twenty, thirty years after unexpected cesareans are still more angry about the cesarean than about any other part of their lives. They still wish they could make the birth go away, make the doctor listen, wave a magic wand to make the past different. The opportunity to heal stays as a permanent guest.

Others, who have begun the process of resolution, balk when a second or third wave of realization hits them concerning how much forgiveness, integration, anger, fear or whatever is their challenge still demands attention.

The issue comes full circle. It began with total denial of the existence of pain, and now there are the same hopes and fears. "You mean I never am free of this?" No, and someday a woman might not want to be. It is part of her, and it makes her whole. Loss and challenge are part of life. Once this realization is acknowledged, a woman must decide what she is doing with that life.

Within her, parts that still feel dead need work: tending, nurturing, mourning, and a fierce determination for protection. That is part of the transformation yet to come. If that work is already done, then a woman knows its value and sees how those elements have become a part of her essential nature.

Forgiveness

Forgiveness happens, but only after fully experiencing and knowing one's feelings and knowing what happened. Even if there is desire to forgive, it won't happen before clearing anger, grief, fear, and sadness.

Forgiveness is a way to integrate the event into one's own life. Instead of the desire to annihilate someone—the doctor, nurse, hospital, or whoever did you harm, the goal is to reconcile that both parties are on the planet together. Any ways to work the conflict out will bear fruit, most importantly for the person doing the forgiving. To change others is not the goal. It is essential to concentrate energies on oneself.

Reconciliation does not necessarily mean that life goes on as before. For example, if an individual is struggling with a doctor, if she writes a letter acknowledging what happened to her and why she was upset, the act of writing the letter is her effort to reach out. She is on her way toward acceptance. The relationship between her and her doctor has changed irrevocably, with new terms and expectations. Even if she chooses to change doctors, she is reconciling that past relationship. She takes strength from her affirming actions and has a new tool for use with relationships.

"Forgive and forget." Where did this phrase come from? It is a nice idea, but unrealistic. "You must forgive and forget" is yet another variation of "What happened wasn't so bad." "I will never forget" is a phrase I hear much more commonly. Trauma is rarely if ever forgotten; it is tempered, instead. The command "to forget" is a strongly used statement that sets up an impossible goal.

"I don't want to forgive" is another commonly heard phrase. Progress does not always look like forgiveness. Vicky is still angry several years after the birth of her first baby. Her actions look unforgiving; they are necessary for acceptance. Vicky states her disagreement about the forgiveness she has learned at church.

What makes me mad, the trouble I have with letting go is why should I have to let this go? Why should I have to stop? Like in church, we're very strict Christian people, and the big thing is forgiving. I am not forgiving Dr. Harvey. I don't care, and Lord, you can do whatever you want to, but I cannot forgive him for that. I do not want to forgive Dr. Harvey, I never will, and I don't see why I should have to.

This is a big point for me, I want to hate him until the day I die, and I want him to burn in hell, and if there is some way I can help him get there . . .

My mother still kisses the ground Dr. Harvey walks on. If I ever went over to her house and he was there, because he has been her doctor for almost thirty years and they also work at the same place, I'd still want to kill him. It's hard to reconcile what is said at church with what I know is right for me. If I forgave him I'd be one big lie.

I've had to go at my own pace. Greg says, "Just forget about it, Vicky. You've had time, now you can forget about it." No, this is my thing, and I'll be done with it when I want to. I don't think it'll ever be gone, I'll never trust a doctor.

Vicky hopes her doctor will burn in hell. She is not very "forgiving" in her thoughts or words toward this doctor. He is at the center of her picture of forgiveness. Vicky has no impulse to forgive; she wants to hang onto her anger instead. That is the direction she needs to go at this time. Though she resists any positive association with the birth of her first baby, she admits that she now knows how to protect herself. This need for protection may be why her anger needs to remain. It provides radar to detect when she is being given the shaft or when she is in danger.

When rage is so huge it feels as though it will never go away, it is hard to believe that forgiveness is an option. Then it is important to remember to give oneself as much time as needed. Keep the feelings flowing, and at a future time, the rage will change, or there will be expanded room to include forgiveness along with the rage. "I am not ready to forgive" is okay.

Forgiveness and acceptance are often confused. Forgiving someone is also often confused with releasing them from responsibility for their actions. Acceptance of what another person did or accepting the reality of the event that happened is closer to feeling a sense of forgiveness, which allows peace of mind. Then whoever or whatever is being forgiven is not being let off the hook and is still responsible for his or her or its own part in the drama.

Forgiveness of oneself is often most difficult. As I release judgment toward myself, I am infinitely more capable of forgiving others. This dynamic was true about cesareans specifically as well as about my audacity to just take up room on the planet. Until I accepted my own cesarean, I had intense judgment of other women who had had them.

My judgment was deep, so I was not totally surprised when four years after the cesarean, I realized that I still blamed my own uterus for not performing as it was supposed to. I shunned that part of me. I could not visualize it as a healthy, vital, warm, vibrant part of me. I couldn't imagine it as an honorable organ in my body. When my periods were painful, I wished I could get rid of my uterus. When it would not conceive right away, I was blaming and punishing toward it. When I had morning sickness, instead of seeing it as a mixed blessing indicating that my hormones were doing their job as well as making me sick, my uterus was once more blackballed. I hated to recall how my uterus was treated during the cesarean and was fearful of the scar, though it had performed beautifully during the subsequent birth. Once I realized my contempt and rage at my uterus—and indeed my uterus isn't a whole person; it is a part of me without ability to speak as we know speech—I was immediately apologetic. I was remorseful at targeting it with so much hostility. I bathed it in praise for all the wonderful work it had done and continues to do. It has birthed two beautiful babies, it works each and every day at maintaining the life cycle, and it sustains life and creates life. I was surprised by this pocket of forgiveness, this piece of healing. I begin to expect these surprises, as the birth continues to unwind through my own life cycle.

If You're Still in Pain: Taking Opportunities to Heal

There would be a core of dread if I had not explored the emotional pain of my first son's birth. I know my capacity to enjoy my children is enhanced and has blossomed—perhaps even exists—because of the healing undergone. I am also sure there are nooks and crannies still deadened that will awaken as I am ready, as events trigger their emergence. A traumatic birth is a lifelong gift, though at times it still seems, and still is, a loss and a negative event. Issues of regret, acceptance, and forgiveness often take a longer time to reconcile than desired.

Ellen was adamant after her first birth about the need to finish with her experiences. She wanted to forgive and move on as quickly as possible.

I've worked through Jason's birth, and I believe there is no purpose to dwelling on it any longer. That would be wallowing, and I've never wanted to be like that.

I believe that you have to go on, that wallowing in pity has no use. I've worked through this issue, and if I have another baby, that will heal me. There is no purpose in going back any more to Jason's birth events.

I find it hard to believe that like you say, I'll keep remembering the birth and need to rehash it. You're right, it was traumatic, there's lots of things that happen in your life, but you've got to play the cards you were dealt.

We negotiated back and forth as I asked her to make more room for Jason's birth. Her nature was to forgive and forget as soon as possible, to get on with her life by counting her blessings. But if she squeezed out any recognition of all the memories and feelings, they would return in other ways. Like a scar that heals, changing shape and color, memories transform over time but remain present. Unlike a scar, it is easier to believe memories can be banished forever. If banishment is attempted, the cost is high, as part of a woman is then severed, like an amputated arm or leg.

Ellen and I finally agreed that to expand to include both points of view would work. A balance point is created, because, as Ellen later said, "If you go too far one way, you will never get over it. And if you go too far the other way and try to forget about it, it will come back to haunt you." Ellen went on to explain the role model she used to get over unpleasant situations.

I'm German, I have a stoic approach. That no matter what you go through, you don't sit around and wallow in it. My maternal grandmother had rheumatoid arthritis, and she had lost movement in her elbows and her knees, and most of the movement in her hips and fingers and ankles. She was my example of how you deal with adversity. She didn't just sit in bed, she got out and mowed the lawn on her riding lawn mower. And baked all kinds of breads and pastries, she still tried to be a productive person. A lot of people would have just given up and been in a wheelchair. But she wasn't so nice to my grandpa, she wouldn't talk to him for two weeks at a time. She created a lot of trauma in my dad's and my uncle's lives, I think because she was consumed with her own problems. Her own unacknowledged problems.

Ellen had an incredible role model for facing adversity, one full of strength and determination. Together with her own experiences, she is finding her own balance point between acknowledging and coping with adversity and denial of its existence.

Healing happens as a woman is open and ready to do the work involved. Like feelings, memories also have lives of their own. I want to finish being angry long before that anger is ready to leave, just as I want to forget what happened. Trying to hurry the situation will produce frustration and a sense of failure at not being done yet.

Every time a piece of insight or resolution is found or another layer of fear is released, relief is experienced and is real. At each of those moments, pause and take satisfaction in the accomplishment. A valuable gift to give oneself is as much time as needed to heal. It represents acceptance of oneself, trusting that when there is a need to heal, the need will be tended to.

After a traumatic birth or after expectations were turned upside down and inside out, a woman is forced to learn some difficult lessons the hard way. At this important time, she would lose something more valuable then precious gems if she tried to deny any part of herself.

FOR WORK ON YOUR OWN

Question One: Are you aware of an entire range of feelings, including fear, anger, whining, grief, joy? Which feeling happens most often? Which feeling happens least often? Does one feeling hide others?

Question Two: Reread all the quotes at the beginning of the chapter. Which ones can you imagine saying, either out loud or to yourself? Now take each quote you noted and decide whether it represents fear, anger, grief, whining, or denial of one of these feelings. Now explore further each particular emotion in relation to the birth or events that occurred afterwards.

Question Three: If you picked colors to represent feelings, what would they be? Choose colors for anger, grief, fear, joy, and whining. What size, shape, density, and texture is each feeling? If this idea generates energy or interest, try painting, drawing, or coloring as you focus on each feeling.

FOR FURTHER READING

Baldwin, Rahima, and Palmarini, Terra. (1986) *Pregnant Feelings.* Berkeley, CA: Celestial Arts.

Bozarth-Campbell, Alla. (1986) *Life Is Goodby, Life Is Hello, Grieving Well through All Kinds of Loss.* Minneapolis, MN: CompCare.

Flanigan, Beverly. (1992) *Forgiving the Unforgivable.* New York: Macmillan.
(Love Is Letting Go of Fear, and *Life's Companion: Journal Writing as a Spiritual Quest* each have chapters on forgiveness.)

Fritsch, Julie, and Ilse, Sherokee. (1988) *The Anguish of Loss.* Maple Plain, MN: Wintergreen Press.

Jampolsky, Gerald. (1989) *Love Is Letting Go of Fear.* New York: Bantam.

Kopp, Sheldon. (1988) *Raise Your Right Hand against Fear: Extend the Other in Compassion*. Minneapolis, MN: CompCare.

Lerner, Harriet. (1989) *Dance of Anger*. New York: HarperCollins.

___. (1990) *Dance of Intimacy: A Woman's Guide to Courageous Acts of Change in Key Relationships*. New York: HarperCollins.

Rubin, Theodore Isaac. (1970) *The Angry Book*. New York: Collier Macmillan.

CREATIVE TOOLS FOR RECOVERY

Over time, knowledge about birth that one can work with will be gained. Sources include previous birth experiences, life events, and strong feelings mined instead of suppressed. Another baby may be considered, and talking with other women about their birth stories broadens one's sphere of healing potential. A woman may be all over the map, with visceral or visual memories, a journal begun, and several valuable books scattered around her. Now is the time to gather sources together in specific tasks. How does this gathering take place?

For several years, my energy poured into written words and water color paintings. I have a series of fifty paintings depicting pregnancy, birth, and life with a small child. Later these subjects included life with two small children. The paintings are primitive. I never took an art class, and more than once a person has commented, "I like that, did a child paint it?" I am not advocating inner child work here; this simplistic style is truly how I paint. My writing began with a journal, then a memoir, and later expanded to include two novels, this book, and more works in progress. These two mediums, painting and writing, have been most satisfying to me. I have knitted my healing onto paper with words, images, and colors. I also crave seeing and hearing others' work; doing so fills me up.

There are countless ways of expression to be claimed as one's own. Any form of expression will cultivate creativity and pull out surprises from deep within. The "For Work on Your Own" sections at the end of each chapter can be pulled out and used as an outline of questions for anyone to make a quilt, in any format, of her healing journey. A literal quilt would be a beautiful way of meditating and sewing together each step of the path. Knitting a sweater, drawing, singing, writing, building a fence or house, planting a garden or tree—any creative act is a transforming agent for a woman invested in her own healing.

Though I outline specific tasks and ideas, the concept of expressing one's creativity as an agent for healing is applicable anywhere, at any time, in any form. The methods in this chapter are ones I know well. Journal writing, dream work, body work, story telling, acknowledging anniversaries, creating ceremonies, and affirmations are included. In addition, what is discussed about journal writing is applicable to other formats, and vice versa. The topics are individually discussed to introduce them with clarity. Please keep in mind the infinite number of creative ways and methods that are available.

WRITING

Journal Writing

If a written account of one's life has never been kept, there are many resources available now to help someone begin. A list of good books on journal writing is included in the reference section, and short courses are often offered through adult or continuing education.

The most important point to remember is this: if there is a desire to write, begin. Anywhere. On any paper. With any word. Grammar, style, whether it will ever be published or read by anyone else—these should not be guiding forces or essential components of writing.

The best lesson I ever learned about creating anything can be applied to all creative processes including those involving pictures and words. It is to fill one page, then turn it. Fill another page, turn that page, and don't look back. Just fill page after page, keep turning, and see what happens next. My ability to be critical is far too developed; if I assess any of my creative work, I freeze. So I keep turning those pages, both while writing and while painting. Days or years later, I pull out a notebook or sketch pad and am able to appreciate and modify the pages. But in the moment, create, and then turn the page.

Having time to write can be a limiting factor. Especially with small children in the house, it is easy to misplace the craving for writing time. Busyness, if not outright chaos, becomes the rule. I know many mothers who write at night, the most easily carved out time, unless day care is an option. The point here is to make an opportunity happen. A friendly kitchen table, a desk in a corner of the hall, a lap with a board placed across, a notebook on one's knees, or a sunny study with a state-of-the-art computer—in any of these places at any hour of the day or night, writing is possible.

Assuming there is now a pen, brush, or chalk in hand, I will explore words specifically about birth.

Birth Story. The most fruitful place to begin is with the birth of one's baby. Write down every detail that is possible to remember. Begin with concrete details. Include time, place, colors, smells, textures, who was there, what was said. Take a rest if needed. The first layer has been completed.

When the task is picked up again, go to the second layer and describe the inner space of birth. What was happening inside of you while all the concrete world continued on the outside. Where was your mind? Was it in the well-lit room, or elsewhere? How were you aware of the baby? What was the baby telling you? What did you say out loud, and what did you say inside yourself?

Especially when exploring the potent and sensitive subject of birth, the need for permission to write without censor is crucial. Once I even wrote out a permission slip to myself. Another time I wrote out a permission slip to be signed by my husband, giving me permission to take time to write. Though unfounded, I felt guilty and fearful that he was angry at me. It read, "Lynn Madsen has my permission to write at any time and for as long as she wants to, forever." I kept it in my sock drawer for years, and would often come across it while rummaging for a matching pair. It always made me smile and feel my power to write. Even if someone is angry with a woman for taking time to write or work on whatever form of expression she needs, making her own permission slip will help. Staking a claim for a time and place to fulfill what she needs to do will make the task achievable.

The act of recording a birthing story is difficult to begin; it may feel like an act of betrayal to all those voices who minimized the heartbreak, depression, pain, or disappointment. Those voices helped reverse the words she needed to express. Those words then became stuck in her throat, or stuffed further into her body. To write about what happened may act as a catalyst, as a key that unlocks and releases her voice and power. It is also scary, because saying or writing the truth means movement and change. Power can be scary. At times like this it is helpful to remember that any effort deserves affirmation, and the words will come as fast or as slow as a woman is ready for them.

"Here is my story!" she then proclaims about her story in whatever form it takes. "It's Mine! No matter what anyone else says, they can't take away these words that I put on paper about what happened to me. If someone else was there, and they believe something else happened, let it go on record that I believe *this* happened."

Letters Never to Be Sent

A fruitful writing task is to write letters that are never intended to be sent. Letters to doctors, nurses, midwives, husbands, parents, friends, sons, daughters, anyone a woman needs to have words with. These uncensored letters are a potent release of the crevices and blocks of lead that are inside of a woman after a negative, disappointing, or traumatic birth.

Visualize the energy of the pain, anger, or other strong emotion flowing down the fingers and out the tip of the pen, onto the paper where it will now reside. The words do not have to make sense. Start with "Dear Nurse Smith," or "Dear sister Ann." If still blocked, try writing with the nondominant hand.

Even though my cesarean was necessary, I still wanted to blow up the hospital, the doctor, the machines, and anyone else remotely connected to that birth. After writing various pieces of my mind to each person involved, after "blowing them all up" figuratively, I no longer carried that desire inside. Although never directly delivered, those responses flowed out with written and spoken words. Eventually I could even drive by the hospital without flashing back to those birth days; I barely gave them a thought.

Writing letters to hospital administrators, the president, the governor, insurance companies, drug companies—think big—also help release powerlessness. Much, much later, when the critic in a woman has subsided, these lovely, powerful, no-holds-barred letters may act as seeds to germinate into new letters that are meant to be sent. But black out these words if they inhibit the beginning efforts. Whatever the final outcome, begin writing and create the crucial outpouring necessary for healing that this writing allows.

Letters Meant to Be Sent

After several moons have passed, and the anger, rage, fear, and whatever else that needs to has erupted, flowed, or oozed out by osmosis as a result of a woman's saying her piece, there may be a need to actually write sendable letters. A well-written letter conveying information about prenatal care, labor and delivery, or postnatal care is valuable information for a doctor, midwife, hospital administrator, or anyone else a woman needs to write to. If a doctor or other caregiver truly wants to improve the care provided, a dialogue may ensue. If a doctor wants no such feedback, this letter will be a distraction, like a buzzing fly that needs to be dealt with—but some women would consider this a small price to extract.

Sending a personal letter provides potential for new communications. There is always the risk that it may have the opposite effect of shutting down communications, but the sender will know where she stands and will have stood up for herself. To reach out in this way can be threatening. The way a relationship functioned in the past may no longer be an option. Friendships, professional relationships, and familial patterns all have the potential of disruption as well as improvement when honest communication occurs.

Expressing such vulnerable parts of oneself is easier when a supportive person is involved. Find someone who is willing to be there when the original letter is sent or call is made; when the response letter is opened and read. Creating one's own safety net of support allows a woman to continue reaching out.

Keep in mind that a woman always knows whether sharing her words is what she needs to do; this action step is not mandatory for healing. Her knowledge about herself is what is crucial. Often recognizing that I am angry at someone, or hurt, or that there is a misunderstanding is most of my work. Then I am capable of making peace, whether or not I have shared any information with the other party. Even if a letter is sent, or another type of reaching out is done, the goal is to state one's case and expand the sphere of influence for oneself. The respondent's reactions are not guaranteed to be satisfying. No change in the status quo is the most likely result.

Each and every time one's story is told or written, each time there is increased clarity in a relationship due to honest communication, the wheel of change begins to roll. Then that individual influences all the rest of us because she herself is changed; we are affected in some way, if not directly.

The "For Work on Your Own" Sections

Go back to the beginning of this book, and peruse all of the questions at the end of each chapter in the "For Work on Your Own" sections. When a question pulls deep inside or creates some kind of movement, use it as a place from which to leap. Create as many words as desired: a sentence, a page, a notebook. Any amount of writing will be effective.

Play with each question. Answer it as though I am sitting across from you. Answer as though your doctor is saying the words. Answer the question chosen as though you are asking yourself. See what different responses occur. Choose other significant persons to imagine responding to.

Any form of writing is an outpouring that will help an individual find her center. It can also open doors to other forms of expression.

DREAM WORK

Many dreams are included in the memoir excerpts. Dreams are an integral part of my day; they are remembered, wondered about, and listened to for the internal messages they give from deep inside. Dreams are the most easily accessible source of one's unconscious. For me to know my dreams is to know myself.

Many people say they don't dream because they don't remember their dreams. They may not remember them, but everyone does dream. Excellent books on how to remember and interpret dreams are included in the reference section. Here, I will provide in a nutshell ways to remember dreams and relate them to aspects of birth, and to the healing process.

To Catch a Dream

To remember dreams, place some sort of recording instrument—pen and paper or a tape recorder—next to where you sleep. Immediacy is essential; when you first awake is the best time to remember dreams. If recorded, they will stay with you. Thinking about a dream isn't enough to remember it; the act of getting out of bed will erase many dreams. The other most helpful way to remember dreams is to program oneself before sleep; tell yourself that you will remember your dream upon waking. This method works, though for some individuals sooner than others. If you are persistent, even if remembering a dream is rare, at least one dream will be in your hands after a few weeks or months.

Pregnancy, Birth, and Dreams

Patricia Maybruck and Patricia Garfield each have books specifically about women's dreams during pregnancy and birth. However, when searching for the meaning behind a specific dream, the dreamer's interpretation of its message is most important, regardless of what a book or an expert says.

If a woman is afraid about the upcoming birth and has no outlet for expressing her fear, then her dreams may take up this important task for her. For example, before Vicky's second birth, she consciously was talking about what she wanted to happen, and she laid careful plans. She knew she did not want to repeat the first birth. When eight months pregnant, she was surprised by a dream.

> I had this dream that I had a c-section, and the baby was back in the room. I said to Greg in the dream, "Put this baby in the corner, and sit with her and love her a lot, because I can't love her, and I can't take care of her. I have no love left in me. My love is gone, so you'll have to love her a lot." I woke up really bothered, I cried for days. I felt so bad that I couldn't love my baby. I said to Greg, "Don't tell anyone about that dream, they'll think that I'm a horrible mother." Then I felt so bad, that this poor baby inside of me is not feeling loved, because I would dream something like this about her. I hoped she didn't know what I was dreaming about. It was really a bad dream.
>
> That week we went to a prenatal exam and the midwife said, "So, have you had any dreams lately?" I said no, and Greg said yes, she has. After going back and forth, I finally told them. I said it was really awful, and I didn't want them to get the wrong opinion. I thought for sure they wouldn't help me with a home birth if they knew I'd hate my baby if I didn't have her vaginally. But I told them the dream. Emily said, "Well, do you know what your dream's about? In some dreams, everybody is you. You're just dreaming that if you had a c-section, you couldn't love yourself any more. Can you deal with that?" And I said, "Yeah," and I felt a little better.
>
> I had coached Greg many times that if we ended up in the hospital to put up signs, "No one enter." Visitors would have to call from the lobby to make sure it was okay to come up. No nurses or doctors could enter without permission. I didn't feel comfortable, it was a safety thing. I didn't want anyone to see me if I had another c-section.

At first, Vicky thought the dream was warning her she would not bond with her baby if it was born cesarean. Not that this fear didn't exist. More important, Vicky realized that the rejection of her newborn baby actually was her fear that she would hate herself if she had another cesarean birth. She had planned on neglecting and withholding love from herself. The new baby left alone in the corner of the room in her dream was how she planned to treat herself, not the baby. Her plans to put up a "No one enter" sign were reevaluated. She recognized the difference between her need for privacy and respect and the support and care she would deserve from friends if the need to have a c-section arose.

The dream was a most valuable gift that helped Vicky to forgive and accept herself. Though she did not have to face the challenge of another cesarean and she did not get to the point where she could accept the possibility of one happening again, she was better prepared with the piece of knowledge the dream provided.

Vicky's is an example of how a dream of giving birth is often about giving birth to oneself. Even when the dreamer is not pregnant, a dream of giving birth can represent the birth of a new part of a person, a project, or a new phase of life. The theme of birth in a dream represents life emerging in any form.

Sometimes after a traumatic birth, after the loss of a baby, or while pregnant, a woman dreams of an ideal birth or an ideal baby. She may feel honored by this dream, or it may spark another wave of grief. After the miscarriage when I lost baby Alice, I dreamed of a beautiful baby girl, born easily. I held her and walked around showing her to all my friends, feeling complete joy. Then I realized the placenta had not come out yet. I returned to the birthing room and tried to push out the placenta, but it would not emerge. When I woke up, I enjoyed the baby girl who visited me in this dream, and also realized I was holding on to the wish that she could still really be born. I wasn't letting go of her, as I didn't let go of the placenta in the dream.

Dreams and Posttraumatic Stress Disorder

When birth trauma has occurred, dreams are actively involved with its clearing. Many women who experience posttraumatic stress disorder (PTSD) due to birth events count persistent dreams as a primary symptom. For some, the dreams persist for years, repeating their urgent messages, needing to be heard. There are also some sleep disorders involving terrifying dreams that I do not discuss, as well as drug-induced dreams. If medication is in use, it is worth finding out its side effects, as dreams of terror can be common.

Regarding PTSD, if a woman is having dreams of an unpleasant or terrifying experience, it helps to view the dream as a message or as a way for the trauma both to become integrated and to leave her. Just like a demanding child, if attention is paid, the child eventually happily wanders off to play on its own. So will a dream stop returning during sleep once its message is heard.

What is the dream's message? If it elicits fear or discomfort, avoidance may be used to avoid its message. Denial is again a useful concept. If a woman tries to deny her dream, it will become stronger until she says what needs to be said, acknowledges what is demanding to be known, and lets her feelings surface. Then she can howl in the wind, use her entire body to smash, or hold herself to comfort her fear. If attempts are made to control her honest reactions to the birth, for example, if she is wishing it had not happened, her dream will continue to fight with her. Although it may feel like a torment or a negative side of herself best forgotten, these dark aspects are a part of her. To accept them as part of the whole person brings peace. A whole person includes the full range of emotions and desires. The only way I know to stop repetitive dreams is to listen to the message. When the dream is so terrifying that it paralyzes a woman so she can't hear the message or work with it, there are techniques to find the message in less threatening forms (see references).

The dream may be a message showing how a woman is berating herself for letting the birth happen, a message pointing out her belief that she deserves punishment. Once this belief is realized, then there is knowledge with which to fight. She does not deserve punishment, and this message, after being carefully listened to, needs to be discarded. Stomp on it, throw it away, and replace it with nourishing and life-affirming messages.

Literal messages are also received in dreams. For example, a dream occurs over and over again about a doctor about to perform an unnecessary cesarean. In this case, a woman may not hold her doctor accountable for his or her actions. The dream tells her the message repeatedly, and if she does not take steps—if she does not change doctors, confront the doctor, or do whatever else she needs to do—then she is at risk for further harm. The dream embodies the threat of mistreatment or neglect; it is a message conveying the need for protection and action.

Perhaps the part of her that she believes has died because of the birth or related loss is trying to come alive again through her dream. That transformation may scare her, but it ultimately means she will grow and live. The part of her that feels dead is most likely made up of her outrage, anger, fear, and grief. Deadening and condensing those feelings served a purpose for a time, allowing a woman to function on a daily basis. But now the dead area needs to expand, the feelings need to flow, burble, and erupt out of her. If she tries to suppress them, dreams are an outlet for an otherwise ticking time bomb.

On the other hand, death may be the dream's message. It may symbolize death of one's expectations and fantasies or death of innocence, childhood, a stage of life. If such death-loss is unacknowledged, the dream's message may portray an actual death of oneself or others to emphasize the message. Imminent physical death is not frequently the message; instead, examine some of the possibilities stated. Certainly when trauma has occurred, nontangible aspects of life are shattered. Try to be open to a dream's message even when it includes the "unthinkable."

It is difficult to say, "Thank you, dream, for the message you give to me" when it seems the dream is providing torture instead of comfort. Yet once more, to acknowledge and release the pain is to heal. Dreams are an empowering tool. They provide links to the unknown or little-known realms of the unconscious, spirit, and dark worlds.

BODY WORK

A helpful tool for healing is some form of body work. Some women seek out massage therapy or other touch therapy, such as rebirthing or cranial-sacral therapy. Dance, karate, or other movements help tap what one's body wants to express. Because much birth trauma is physical, and emotional trauma is held in the physical body, attention on the physical plane is a valuable key to fitting all the pieces of one's healing puzzle together. The main focus of this book is on emotional healing, and for many women, body therapy is the only way to retrieve their internal information or feelings. This aspect of healing is the most nontraditional, and there are few references to its benefits found in the library or elsewhere. However, some therapists refer clients for massage or other body therapies. If pursued, body work may shorten the time needed for healing as well as increase the benefits.

STORY TELLING

When my first son was two months old I had a memorable tea party. A friend helped me organize the morning by calling others and planning food and a ceremony. My husband took the baby out for the morning so the house was completely ours. Friends arrived, we gathered in a circle and began with blessings for us all, of friendship, truth, and love. Then I told my birth story, for as long as I wished, with as many details as I wished to tell, and with any expression. With friends around me, the story poured out. Afterwards they all responded with care and praise, we sang a song, and then we ate. I used my heirloom china, and we drank tea and had treats.

This story-telling tea included much ritual and celebration, yet the heart of the event was the story. It has since been told many times. Yet this first telling was so complete, so well listened to, that its power still remains with me. Many seeds of confidence were planted. The power of spoken words and the meaning of community in which to share them were enhanced.

Although support groups are not easily available in every city or state, for many women they are an option. International Cesarean Awareness Network (ICAN, formerly Cesarean Prevention Movement) has chapters in most states, and their meetings are a place to find willing listeners. That organization also welcomes any woman who has an interest in improving her birth experiences; if a cesarean is not the issue, ICAN is still a valuable resource. Some birth clinics offer aftercare groups, and they can also be tried out. Some therapists and birth educators specialize in this topic, although in some areas they are rare to find. And a good friend is invaluable. The issue of whom a woman seeks to tell her story to is vital. An open, willing ear is essential for a story to pour out as needed.

Hearing others' stories is also a vital part of healing. Vicky thought she was "the only person in the world who had an unnecessary cesarean." She felt enormous relief in finding out others had struggled as she was struggling, and she found strength from knowing they had healed.

Telling the Birth Story to Your Baby

When talking about being angry at God or another powerful entity or about what occurred during birth, there often also exists an anger felt toward the baby that is as strong or stronger. Expressing that anger in a safe context is essential. Fear that the baby may be hurt by a mother's anger often prohibits expression. Uncontrollable rage is infinitely different from a clear expression of anger, giving words the power to clear the air. If anger exists, a baby will be aware of it. Expression will release the anger, and then mother and baby can become closer.

When my first son Evan was six months old, even though he was obviously preverbal, I held him in my arms and told him my side of the story. I also admitted how angry I was about how he was born.

"How can you hate your child, this small, defenseless baby, innocent and beautiful, for being the reason for your pain?" I whispered to myself.

"Well, I do—and I have to tell you this, Evan, so it doesn't keep me from you. And it would. I don't care what 'reasons' you had, even that you had to be born by cesarean in order to survive.

I'm still mad that it all happened." I carried him, fussy, around the living room while speaking the words out loud. I went over all the details, and took out the journal I had written for him in the hospital and read passages. I told him about the operating room, the days afterwards. He had the stomach flu that day, each time he threw up another load of laundry would go in the washer. After telling him I was angry, taking care of him was easier. He was just being fussy, and I could handle that. I felt lighter. Now there were no secrets.

Acknowledging anger broke down a barrier. I felt more care and love after its release. If I had continued to try to protect him from any anger, it would have festered within me and between us. I also needed to honor his story and not hide it. If I never spoke about his birth, he would wonder and possibly think something was wrong. Like children do, he would blame himself for my discomfort about his birth. Our dialogue broke many taboos for me—that I had something to hide, that his birth was too painful to discuss, and myriad other negative beliefs that could produce skeletons in the closet. If I were too ashamed of my baby's birth, what would I be able to share with him about his birth story? Even though this first time he didn't understand the words, he understood the meaning, and the barrier of silence between us disappeared.

Later, when Evan was verbal and asked about his birth, especially after his brother was born, I told him the facts. I didn't compare the two births; I stated how each of them was born. "Kyle came out of my vagina, and you came out here, where the doctor cut me open." "Why?" he asked. "Because you weren't getting enough air, and you needed to be born this way so you could live." As time goes by and Evan asks more questions, I will answer them.

Birthdays are often used as an opportunity to focus on a child's birth story, the tale told and embellished with pictures. When a birthday is a celebration, and the birth story is told, the child and mother both have an opportunity to celebrate the actual birth. Even though the journey may have been rocky or worse, they are both here now to share the story.

When an unnecessary cesarean or other violating birth story is related, it is vital for a woman to pass on to her child the empowerment she has since learned, so the child does not inherit her shame or fear. Story telling between a mother and child about birth opens the way to acceptance; then both can move on more easily. Celebrations become possible. To achieve this serenity, any negative anniversary reactions must also be acknowledged before celebrations can occur.

ACKNOWLEDGING ANNIVERSARIES

Anniversaries often are more potent than we realize. They embody uncountable associations that trigger unbidden memories and feelings, desired or not. The time of year alone holds this power. For many mothers, a child's birthday will always bring back memories of his or her birth. My son's first birthday in particular held this power for me.

Tension flooded my body, felt rigid like stone as Evan's first birthday approached in late March. Darkness hung behind my eyes, in my brain, everywhere I looked were vivid memories of the birth. I fought with Michael about totally unrelated events. We planned a party for Evan, but all I could do was make a cake and show up. I felt like a puppet, grateful for others' direction. *Oh—yes, of course, now we open presents. Let's light the candle—darn, he doesn't care, he doesn't even like cake! Yes, he's just beginning to walk, though he was climbing the stairs at eight months. What a great book! What's that you say, horn lessons to go with it in five years? I'll be calling you. Is it over yet?*

I wanted to celebrate his birth, but that day was like trying to run through mud. Someday he would love hearing about his birth—the excitement, how special he is. But I wasn't able to tell it that day without crying and wailing.

Living through that first anniversary made clear again how I needed to forgive myself for what happened. I was still enormously judgmental, and condemned every woman who had ever had a cesarean. I couldn't stop condemning them until I stopped condemning myself.

Evan's birthday was like a heavy storm of rain, thunder, and darkness. When the day was over, there was a fresh, new scent, the earth was washed clean. The storm happened, and then the day became clear. Just like that.

As the years have gone by, I always use the opportunity of my son's birthday to remember. That first year was the hardest, and the memories were most vivid. Now, as his fifth birthday approaches, I will use this opportunity to pause and remember, not to inflict pain, but to mark the occasion as important. I heal still, each time I remember his birth, each time I hear a similar story.

If a strong reaction occurs for no apparent reason, look at the calendar and note if there is a forgotten anniversary. One's body remembers and marks the occasion. Like an important dream, if attention is paid, the anniversary will do its job and then go its own way. Fall is the anniversary of my miscarriage, and this past year I forgot, until one week I was upset and weepy and grieving for no apparent reason. Then the puzzle fit into place. It was the anniversary of Alice's birth and death.

Over time, grief will lessen and will happen less frequently. It always returns, like a little spike on a graph rather than a solid peak, but it will return. A woman grieves or releases terror until she feels entirely empty. A year or two later, those feelings return as though the event happened yesterday, but they last a much shorter time. An anniversary is a way to formalize this process.

The paradox is that if permission is given to pay attention to and remember the trauma or loss, room is then created for the celebration that is desired. As with any feeling, if suppression is attempted, the effects of the trauma will grow stronger and more insistent. If a woman states that she will not remember her baby's birth because she doesn't want to spoil the birthday party, this attempt may boomerang. On Jack's first birthday, Vicky didn't want to remember what happened, partly because she had heard about what a difficult day it had been for me when Evan turned one year old.

> When Jack turned one, I didn't let myself remember it was the anniversary of his birth because you said that first birthday was really bad. I thought, I've got to get this all out of my system before that day, or after that day, because I'm not going to have a bad time on Jack's birthday. We had a great party, but that night at the stroke of midnight I called and had Dr. Harvey paged. He called back, and I said, "Are you doing any unnecessary c-sections this year?" He said, "Who is this?" I said, "You know who I am," then I hung up. The next day I sent a dozen black balloons to his office. They said something like, "Happy hell day, love Jack and Vicky." That day he called back every hour, he or his nurse. My mom or Greg answered the phone. I always thought he would try to sue me for opening my mouth. I don't know how he legally could, I've never made his name public. But I think he's afraid.

Vicky's reaction was strong and vitriolic, and is not necessarily recommended. Obviously her efforts at suppression did not work; if she had been more direct, she might have received more satisfaction. Or perhaps not. Remember, affirmation is needed for any steps toward healing. Steps are not always perfect or appropriate. Vicky's steps were loud and strong.

If time is allotted for remembering, a wellspring of energy is found to make the day one of celebration. For example, a mother may get up early the morning of her baby's birthday and go through pictures, letters, journals, or her memories, and give the day its due. Then she can go on to celebrate, less encumbered. If she needed and took considerably more time for this process, then she has taken care of herself excellently, and she will be a healthy mother and woman as a result.

CREATING CEREMONIES

If there is a need to create an important occasion, a ceremony works. A christening or naming ceremony is a clear example of how valuable a ceremony is. It states that there is a new person in the world, that this is his or her name, and that we are all here to nurture and help this new being grow. Family and friends gather to celebrate, to eat and drink the goodness of life with all their senses.

On a more somber note, some ceremonies are also very effective when a stuffed emotion or particularly difficult memory is causing pain. One event used with Judy, from chapter 1, is particularly simple and powerful. Judy and I met at a county park one afternoon, equipped with paper, wood, water, and matches. Judy described her experience.

Although I felt a little embarrassed, I figured no harm could be done from this meeting, so I gave it a try. First we made a small fire; it was March and still cold outside, so it was nice to have the warmth. Then I wrote on this huge piece of butcher's paper. There was a whole roll of it, so I could write as big as I wanted to. I wrote what I was angry about. At first all I could write, as I used big markers of all different colors, were the words "angry-mad-hate." Big letters. Scribbled. Then, with some coaxing, I wrote "I am angry." Then I wrote what I was specifically angry about. Really mad at the doctor. At all of the parts of the operation.

Then came some harder parts. I was angry at my daughter Kristin for being born by cesarean. That was really hard. I was angry at other people, too. At my husband, at my parents. At his parents. All that hatred toward my body, how I wanted to rip myself open sometimes, I drew on the paper.

Then I realized I was angry at God. God should not have let this happen. God should have helped me more. God screwed up. Then I went wild with the markers, scribbling for about six feet.

When I was finished, I began to tear up all this long paper. I crumpled it up and watched it burn. I cried, and realized some things as it burned. I realized that I had not bonded with Kristin very much. That caused great pain, and I was overcome with grief. But

mostly I watched the ashes float up and felt free. I was lighter.
We watched the fire for a while. Then, like a baptism, I was
sprinkled with water, my hands were washed in the water, and I
drank some water. Then we put out the fire. The whole thing only
took about an hour.

Judy was able to express more freely and expansively in an out-
door environment with physical props to work with. She released energy by manipulating words and paper, by using fire and water. Her
desire to destroy was channeled into this ceremony and transformed
into expression. She no longer was at risk for hurting herself or others
with strong feelings that could have emerged indirectly.

After any birth, a ceremony is useful to mark the end of pregnancy for a variety of purposes. A new mother may feel empty, and her
good-by is a way to mark the loss of pregnancy and to welcome her new
role as a mother. If this was her last baby, she might want to say good-
by to her intent to bear children and mark the passage into a new stage
of life. If she feels wounded from the birth, a ceremony marks the
beginning of her healing journey. If she feels isolated with a new baby
and fearful of her future, she can have a celebration or ceremony to
begin her connection with friends in a new way. She is now a mother
and part of a new family.

We had saved the placenta in the freezer from my first son's
birth. When he was a month old, as a new family we went to a wild
place and buried it in the earth. Though I had not watched the placenta leave my body, I got to return it to the earth. The placenta represented what I had lost as well as a part of what I received. Both my
husband and I stated our hopes for the future as well as our good-bys
to the pregnancy and birth. That afternoon in the sun was one step-
ping-stone to recovery, not a miracle healing. But one stone placed at
a time has led me here, to a point when I feel whole.

USING AFFIRMATIONS

Every woman reconciles her experiences differently. For some, a
traumatic birth unravels many parts of life. Marriage, career, and family relations are all reevaluated, and sometimes destroyed in order to
rebuild on a new foundation created by what has been discovered.
Others take trauma in stride, coping with the healing process as a
companion to an intact life. If birth tapped deeper issues of abuse,
opportunity exists as this door has been opened to begin or enhance
healing. Others respond by separating from their bodies further, per-

haps gaining a large amount of weight or feeling numb. This response need not be judged; a woman has her own time for healing. Opportunity will come again when she is ready.

The best consequences or steps of action as a result of healing vary immensely. Vicky may never willingly go to a hospital or doctor, and she has found her peace in giving birth at home to her second baby. In contrast, I may always need the safety net of a hospital setting in which to give birth. The specter of my first son's birth won't fade; this history heightens my need for early and frequent reassurance of a healthy fetal heartbeat. The availability of technology, which saved my first son's life, provides reassurance, so that I can let go and trust my body. I have no doubt that if I were faced with a home birth as my only option, I would find other and deeper ways to trust. But I don't know if this will be accomplished in this lifetime, just as Vicky doesn't know if she will ever be able to trust a doctor again. Her safety net is created by being away from technology and a hospital.

Ellen has chosen to focus her energy on education and informing other women of the risks and options of giving birth. She may never have the opportunity to give birth naturally, and so her reconciliation occurs emotionally and intellectually, and by affirming her body in other ways.

> Another way I have resolved this birth is knowing that I did the very best I could given the circumstances. If I have the opportunity, I will do it very differently next time. During my first delivery the medical staff did do all those things to me, but I let them. Early on I could have done many things to have changed the situation. I could have gone home instead of having my waters broken, but I was so stuck on getting to sleep, I didn't realize what the next steps would mean. Or I could have refused any of the early interventions, but by the time the epidural was in place, it was too late. I realize all this now, and these are some of the things I would do differently given another opportunity. I would yell a lot louder and a lot sooner. Another way I resolved my anger was to get involved with educating other women so that these kinds of things don't have to happen to them.

Ellen began volunteer work with a pronursing organization and a lobbying group for promoting natural births. She continues to seek health care for herself and her family from caregivers who respect her wishes and her need for information.

Every time there is a twinge of pain, regardless of how much time has passed after the birth, there is an opportunity for healing. One way to enhance healing at any time is to use an affirmation. Affirmations are words written and spoken out loud with a message to promote life and health. All words of an affirmation are positive; a double negative won't work, as our unconscious minds hear the negative regardless of how it is framed.

Affirmations are most effective if repeated several times a day. This technique provides enough reinforcement to absorb the message. Then one's body and mind begin acting on the positive message; they act as though it is true, and it becomes true. Often one-sentence affirmations are used. On a slip of paper taped to the refrigerator or carried in one's pocket, an affirmation can be placed anywhere for easy access and used to fill whatever void needs filling. The following affirmations are a place to begin; they can be modified an infinite number of ways to suit individual needs and desires.

I accept myself just as I am. I completely accept how my baby was born. I embrace my baby's birth as the sacred and precious gift that it is. I trust my ability to heal physically, emotionally, and spiritually. I value my scars as evidence of my life and willingness to know my own self.

I am blessed with a womb that creates babies. I have opportunity to grow because I am a woman. I hold life within me that is precious. I love my body. I love my uterus. I love every cell of my body. I am a whole person. Body, mind, and spirit are completely connected. I thank my body for all that it does for me each day. My body pulses with life.

I embrace all feelings as valuable. I allow pain to flow through me and give its message. I have room within for all feelings.

I am connected with my child; he/she is part of me and part of my daily life. I am free to say whatever is on my mind to members of my family at any time. I ask for and receive support for my life goals. I take risks when I know it is the right choice for me. I love my life.

I wish for healing and kindness and strength for every woman.

FOR FURTHER READING

Healing Imagery

Gawain, Shakti. (1986) *Living in the Light*. Berkeley, CA: Whatever Press.
Hay, Louise. (1985) *You Can Heal Your Life*. Santa Monica, CA: Hay House.

Jones, Carl. (1988) *Visualizations for an Easier Childbirth.* Minneapolis, MN: Meadowbrook.

Shuman, Sandra. (1989) *Source Imagery: Releasing the Power of Your Creativity.* New York: Doubleday.

Siegel, Bernie. (1986) *Love, Medicine and Miracles.* New York: Harper & Row.

Story Telling

Armstrong, Penny, and Feldman, Sheryl. (1990) *A Wise Birth.* New York: Morrow.

Asford, Janet Isaacs, ed. (1984) *Birth Stories: The Experience Remembered.* Trumansburg, NY: The Crossing Press.

Duerk, Judith. (1989) *Circle of Stones: Woman's Journey to Herself.* San Diego, CA: LuraMedia.

Dwinell, Jane. (1992) *Birth Stories: Mystery, Power, and Creation.* Westport, CT: Bergin & Garvey.

Finger, Anne. (1990) *Past Due: A Story of Disability, Pregnancy and Birth.* Seattle, WA: Seal Press.

Gaskin, Ina May. (1977) *Spiritual Midwifery.* Summertown, TN: Book Publishing Co.

Richards, Lynn Baptisti. (1987) *Vaginal Birth after Cesarean.* Westport, CT: Bergin & Garvey.

Towle, Alexandra, ed. (1988) *Mothers.* New York: Simon & Schuster.

Young, Catherine, ed. (Published quarterly) *The Compleat Mother Magazine.* Minot, ND.

Dreams

Breen, Dana. (1989) *Talking with Mothers.* London: Free Association Press.

Faraday, Ann. (1974) *The Dream Game.* New York: Perennial Library.

____. (1986) *Dream Power.* New York: Berkley.

Garfield, Patricia. (1988) *Women's Bodies, Women's Dreams.* New York: Ballantine.

Maybruck, Patricia. (1989) *Pregnancy and Dreams.* Los Angeles: Jeremy Tarcher Press.

Journal Writing

Baldwin, Christina. (1990) *Life's Companion: Journal Writing as a Spiritual Quest*. New York: Bantam.

_____. (1991, 1977) *One to One: Self-Understanding through Journal Writing*. New York: M. Evans and Company.

Finlayson, Judith. (1992) *A Book of One's Own: A Journal for Women in Search of Themselves*. New York: Crown.

Goldberg, Natalie. (1986) *Writing Down the Bones*. Boston, MA: Shambhala.

_____. (1990) *Wild Mind*. New York: Bantam.

Hagan, Kay Leigh. (1990, 1988) *Internal Affairs: A Journalkeeping Workbook for Self-Intimacy*. San Francisco: Harper & Row.

Rico, Gabrielle Lusser. (1986) *Writing the Natural Way: Using Right Brain Techniques to Release Your Expressive Power*. Los Angeles: Tarcher/Houghton Mifflin.

Ueland, Brenda. (1938, 1983) *If You Want to Write*. Minneapolis, MN: The Schubert Club.

REFERENCES

BODY IMAGE

Borysenko, Joan. (1987) *Minding the Body, Mending the Mind.* New York: Bantam.
____. (1990) *Guilt Is the Teacher, Love Is the Lesson.* New York: Warner.
Chernin, Kim. (1982) *The Obsession: Reflections on the Tyranny of Slenderness.* New York: Harper Colophon.
Freeman, Rita. (1988). *Bodylove.* New York: Harper & Row.
Hutchinson, Marcia. (1985) *Transforming Body Image.* Trumansburg, NY: The Crossing Press.
Wolf, Naomi. (1991) *The Beauty Myth: How Images of Beauty Are Used Against Women.* New York: Morrow.

CESAREAN INFORMATION

Cohen, Nancy. (1991) *Open Season: A Survival Guide for Natural Childbirth and VBAC in the 90s.* Westport, CT: Bergin & Garvey.
Cohen, Nancy Wainer, and Estner, Lois. (1983) *Silent Knife: Cesarean Prevention and Vaginal Birth after Cesarean (VBAC).* Westport, CT: Bergin & Garvey.
Jones, Carl. (1987) *Birth without Surgery: A Guide to Preventing Unnecessary Cesareans.* New York: Dodd, Mead.
Marieskind, Helen. (1972) *An Evaluation of Cesarean Section in the United States: A Report to the Department of Health, Education and Welfare.* Washington, D.C.: Department of Health, Education, and Welfare.

Peterson, Gayle, and Mehl, Louis. (1985) *Cesarean Birth: Risk and Culture*. Berkeley, CA: Mindbody.
VanTuinen, Ingrid, and Wolfe, Sidney. (1992) *Unnecessary Cesarean Sections: Halting a National Epidemic*. Washington, D.C.: Public Citizen's Research Group.

DREAMS

Breen, Dana. (1989) *Talking with Mothers*. London: Free Association Press.
Faraday, Ann. (1974) *The Dream Game*. New York: Perennial Library.
____. (1986) *Dream Power*. New York: Berkley.
Garfield, Patricia. (1988) *Women's Bodies, Women's Dreams*. New York: Ballantine.
Maybruck, Patricia. (1989) *Pregnancy and Dreams*. Los Angeles: Jeremy Tarcher Press.

EMOTIONAL ASPECTS OF BIRTH

Baldwin, Rahima, and Palmarini, Terra. (1986) *Pregnant Feelings*. Berkeley, CA: Celestial Arts.
Kitzinger, Sheila. (1984) *The Experience of Childbirth*. New York: Penguin.
____. (1989) *Giving Birth*. New York: Noonday.
Noble, Elizabeth. (1983) *Childbirth with Insight*. Boston: Houghton Mifflin.
Panuthos, Claudia. (1984) *Transformation through Birth*. Westport, CT: Bergin & Garvey.
Peterson, Gayle. (1991) *An Easier Childbirth: A Workbook for Pregnant Women*. Los Angeles: Jeremy Tarcher Press.
The following three texts are a series:
Peterson, Gayle. (1984) *Birthing Normally*. Berkeley, CA: Mindbody Press.
____. (1985) *Pregnancy as Healing*. Berkeley, CA: Mindbody Press.
Peterson, Gayle, and Mehl, Louis. (1985) *Cesarean Birth: Risk and Culture*. Berkeley, CA: Mindbody.
Ray, Sondra. (1986) *Ideal Birth*. Berkeley, CA: Celestial Arts.
Simkin, Penny. (1992) "Overcoming the Legacy of Childhood Sexual Abuse: The Role of Caregivers and Childbirth Educators." *Birth Journal: Issues in Perinatal Care 19*. Cambridge, MA: Scientific Publications.

GENERAL PREGNANCY AND BIRTH INFORMATION

Jones, Carl. (1988) *The Birth Partner's Handbook*. Minneapolis, MN: Meadowbrook.
____. (1989) *Sharing Birth: A Father's Guide to Giving Support during Labor*. Westport, CT: Bergin & Garvey.
Kitzinger, Sheila. (1987) *Your Baby, Your Way: Making Pregnancy Decisions and Birth Plans*. New York: Pantheon.
____. (1991) *Homebirth*. New York: Dorling Kindersley.
Korte, Diana, and Scaer, Roberta. (1992) *A Good Birth, a Safe Birth*. Boston: Harvard Common Press.
Lesko, Wendy, and Lesko, Matthew. (1984) *The Maternity Sourcebook*. New York: Warner.
Odent, Michel. (1992) *The Nature of Birth and Breastfeeding*. Westport, CT: Bergin & Garvey.
Simkin, Penny. (1989) *The Birth Partner: Everything You Need to Know to Help a Woman through Childbirth*. Boston: Harvard Common Press.

HEALING IMAGERY

Gawain, Shakti. (1986) *Living in the Light*. Berkeley, CA: Whatever Press.
Hay, Louise. (1985) *You Can Heal Your Life*. Santa Monica, CA: Hay House.
Jones, Carl. (1988) *Visualizations for an Easier Childbirth*. Minneapolis, MN: Meadowbrook.
Shuman, Sandra. (1989) *Source Imagery: Releasing the Power of Your Creativity*. New York: Doubleday.
Siegel, Bernie. (1986) *Love, Medicine and Miracles*. New York: Harper & Row.

INFANT LOSS

Bozarth-Campbell, Alla. (1986) *Life Is Goodby, Life Is Hello, Grieving Well through All Kinds of Loss*. Minneapolis, MN: CompCare.
Feinstein, David, and Mayo, Peg Elliott. (1990) *Rituals for Living and Dying: How We Can Turn Loss and the Fear of Death into an Affirmation of Life*. San Francisco: HarperCollins.
Fritsch, Julie, and Ilse, Sherokee. (1988) *The Anguish of Loss*. Maple Plain, MN: Wintergreen Press.

Ilse, Sherokee. (1982) *Empty Arms: A Guide to Help Parents and Loved Ones Cope with Miscarriage, Stillbirth, and Neonatal Death.* Maple Plain, MN: Wintergreen Press.
____. (1989) *Presenting Unexpected Outcomes: A Childbirth Educator's Guide.* Maple Plain, MN: Wintergreen Press.
Ilse, Sherokee, and Burns, Linda Hammer. (1985) *Miscarriage: A Shattered Dream.* Maple Plain, MN: Wintergreen Press.
Levine, Stephen. (1987) *Healing into Life and Death.* New York: Anchor Books.
Panuthos, Claudia, and Romeo, Catherine. (1984) *Ended Beginnings: Healing Childbearing Losses.* New York: Warner Books.

JOURNAL WRITING

Baldwin, Christina. (1990) *Life's Companion: Journal Writing as a Spiritual Quest.* New York: Bantam.
Finlayson, Judith. (1992) *A Book of One's Own: A Journal for Women in Search of Themselves.* New York: Crown.
Goldberg, Natalie. (1986) *Writing Down the Bones.* Boston: Shambhala.
____. (1990) *Wild Mind.* New York: Bantam.
Hagan, Kay Leigh. (1990, 1988) *Internal Affairs: A Journalkeeping Workbook for Self-Intimacy.* San Francisco: Harper & Row.
Rico, Gabrielle Lusser. (1986) *Writing the Natural Way: Using Right Brain Techniques to Release Your Expressive Power.* Los Angeles: Tarcher/Houghton Mifflin.
Ueland, Brenda. (1938, 1983) *If You Want to Write.* Minneapolis, MN: The Schubert Club.

MEDICAL TRAINING AND INFORMATION

American Psychiatric Association. (1987) *DSM-III-R: Diagnostic and Statistical Manual, Third Edition, Revised.* Washington, D.C.: American Psychiatric Association.
Dalton, Katharina. (1989) *Depression after Childbirth: How to Recognize and Treat Postnatal Illness.* Oxford, UK: Oxford University Press.
Harrison, Michelle. (1982) *A Woman in Residence.* New York: Random House.
Herman, Judith. (1992) *Trauma and Recovery: The Aftermath of Violence —from Domestic Abuse to Political Terror.* New York: Basic Books.

Jack, Dana Crowley. (1991) *Silencing the Self: Women and Depression.* Cambridge, MA: Harvard University Press.
Pekkanen, John. (1988) *M.D. Doctors Talk about Themselves.* New York: Delacorte.

MYTHOLOGICAL, PHILOSOPHICAL, AND HISTORICAL BIRTH REFERENCES

Arms, Suzanne. (1975) *Immaculate Deception.* Boston: Houghton Mifflin.
Capra, Fritjof. (1982) *The Turning Point: Science, Society, and the Rising Culture.* New York: Simon & Schuster.
Davis-Floyd, Robbie. (1992) *Birth as an American Rite of Passage.* Berkeley: University of California Press.
Gray, Elizabeth Dodson, ed. (1988) *Sacred Dimensions of Women's Experience.* Wellesley, MA: Roundtable Press.
Mitford, Jessica. (1992) *The American Way of Birth.* New York: Dutton.
Perera, Sylvia Brinton. (1981) *Descent to the Goddess: A Way of Initiation for Women.* Toronto: Inner City Books.
Starhawk. (1989) *The Spiral Dance.* New York: HarperCollins.

POSTPARTUM ADJUSTMENT

Cowan, Carolyn, and Cowan, Philip. (1992) *When Partners Become Parents.* New York: Basic Books.
Crosby, Faye. (1991) *Juggling: The Unexpected Advantages of Balancing Career and Home for Women and Their Families.* New York: Free Press.
Goldman, Katherine. (1993) *My Mother Worked and I Turned Out Okay.* New York: Villard.
Sanders, Darcie, and Bullen, Martha. (1992) *Staying Home: From Full-Time Professional to Full-Time Parent.* Boston: Little, Brown.
Sanford, Linda, and Donovan, Mary Ellen. (1984) *Women and Self-Esteem.* New York: Penguin.
Sears, William. (1985) *The Fussy Baby: How to Bring Out the Best in Your High-Need Child.* Minneapolis, MN: La Leche.

STORY TELLING

Armstrong, Penny, and Feldman, Sheryl. (1990) *A Wise Birth*. New York: Morrow.

Asford, Janet Isaacs, ed. (1984) *Birth Stories: The Experience Remembered*. Trumansburg, NY: The Crossing Press.

Duerk, Judith. (1989) *Circle of Stones: Woman's Journey to Herself*. San Diego, CA: LuraMedia.

Dwinell, Jane. (1992) *Birth Stories: Mystery, Power, and Creation*. Westport, CT: Bergin & Garvey.

Finger, Anne. (1990) *Past Due: A Story of Disability, Pregnancy and Birth*. Seattle, WA: Seal Press.

Gaskin, Ina May. (1977) *Spiritual Midwifery*. Summertown, TN: Book Publishing Co.

Richards, Lynn Baptisti. (1987) *Vaginal Birth after Cesarean*. Westport, CT: Bergin & Garvey.

Towle, Alexandra, ed. (1988) *Mothers*. New York: Simon & Schuster.

Young, Catherine, ed. (Published quarterly) *The Compleat Mother Magazine*. Minot, ND.

OTHER SELF-KNOWLEDGE TOOLS

Flanigan, Beverly. (1992) *Forgiving the Unforgivable*. New York: Macmillan.

Forward, Susan. (1989) *Toxic Parents: Overcoming Their Hurtful Legacy and Reclaiming Your Life*. New York: Bantam Books.

Jampolsky, Gerald. (1989) *Love Is Letting Go of Fear*. New York: Bantam.

Kasl, Charlotte Davis. (1989) *Women, Sex, and Addiction: A Search for Love and Power*. New York: Ticknor & Fields.

Kaufman, Gershen, and Raphael, Lev. (1983) *The Dynamics of Power*. Cambridge, MA: Schenkman.

Lerner, Harriet. (1989) *Dance of Anger*. New York: HarperCollins.

____. (1990) *Dance of Intimacy: A Woman's Guide to Courageous Acts of Change in Key Relationships*. New York: HarperCollins.

Miller, Alice. (1984) *Thou Shalt Not Be Aware*. New York: Meridian/Penguin.

Orr, Leonard, and Ray, Sondra. (1978) *Rebirthing in the New Age*. Berkeley, CA: Celestial Arts.

Sanford, Linda. (1990) *Strong at the Broken Places*. New York: Random House.

INDEX

Vicky, 36, 122, 145
  birthday reaction and, 148
  dreams and, 141-42
  first birth, 25-32
  forgiveness and, 129-30
  postpartum adjustment and,
    77-78
  releasing fear and, 115-16
  second birth, 106-8
  support from mother and,
    46-47
  support from spouse and,
    43-45

whining, 89, 123-25
A Wise Birth (Armstrong and
    Feldman), 92
work, 69-72, 74, 79-87
  need for flexibility in, 79
  homemaker, conflict with, 79,
    80, 84-85
writing. *See* journal writing;
    letter writing

Your Baby Your Way (Kitzinger), 36

About the Author

LYNN MADSEN is a psychologist who specializes in traumatic birth experiences in the Minneapolis area. She is a journalist and writes from her personal experiences as a three-time mother.